29 1/2 YEARS OF MARRIAGE

29 1/2 YEARS OF MARRIAGE

I was married to a preacher who was a pimp/conartist/player

Ruth J. Webb

To order additional copies of this book, contact:
Xlibris Corporation
1-888-795-4274
www.Xlibris.com
Orders@Xlibris.com
38919

CONTENTS

Special Thanks

To the reader, thank you for selecting my autobiography to read. I pray that you will receive strength and encouragement from it.

We all have a story to tell; some may seem more horrible than others, but still, we all have something to share. I just felt led to share my story with you.

I am not sharing about myself for anyone to feel sorry for me nor am I doing it so the devil can get glory, but that my God and Father, Jesus Christ can and will be glorified.

I felt as if I had been to hell and back, as if I really know what that feels like to go to hell. No one would ever know the pain and torment that I experienced from another human being; it was utterly appalling.

I can say today that through it all, through every name-calling, every fist in my face, slap upside my head and over my body the Lord Jesus Christ was with me. I was kicked, choked, slapped. But God! He even used his mouth by biting, and spitting on me like I was some dog. But by the grace of God I made it! Thank God, I made it!

If the devil would have had it his way he would have had me dead or in a crazy house somewhere pulling out my hair and playing with my lips, oh but God had plans for me. I am so appreciative to God for bringing me out alive. To God I will forever be grateful.

God was with me all the time, even when He didn't seem as though He was, He was! He was right there leading and guiding me and catching all my tears. He gave me the strength to go on. The Lord told me I shall live, and I believed Him.

He gave me the strength to rise up another day. When the enemy would speak to me and tell me to take my own life because no one loves me or cares, God was there with His still soft voice saying, "Daughter you shall live and not die". If I did not know Jesus Christ as my personal savior, I know I would be dead in my grave today. Satan has been trying to snatch my life away from me ever since I came into this world because God has a calling on my life. I have decided to accept His calling and the devil is mad!

But with God on my side, I win!

In this book I share different parts of my life that I don't think would ever be erased. I didn't say I would not ever forgive. I have to forgive and with God's help He has allowed me to be able to forgive and put it behind me. I have forgiven them both, even though I was made to feel like I did not deserve to be alive. But Glory to God! I am free!

I had to forgive myself and I did, I had to love myself and let me tell you, I do.

I want to share the hurt, wounds and pain that I suffered with others in hopes that God will deliver someone. I am a witness that God is no respect of persons, what He has done for one He will do the same for others.

Rejoice with others when they rejoice, and be sorrowful with others when they are hurting and your season will come and you too will shine.

This is for all those hurting men, women and children and even those that never had to experience this kind of lifestyle. To everyone that is being abused by someone or something, know that God is a deliver and He will deliver you.

Thank you!

Acknowledgments

I would like to thank my dear husband, Pastor Clarence T. Webb, who believed in me. Thank you honey for your patience, and for the time you allowed me to spend writing my book. It was because of your support I was able to complete my book. You were concerned about my rest, staying up those late nights and early mornings sitting at the computer as I relived that horrible ordeal. God has truly blessed me.

To my wonderful children, Alfonzo, Kima, Tisha & my stepdaughter, Brandie: To my nine lovely precious grandchildren, I appreciate all of you for loving me and being there for me. I love you.

I must also thank my spiritual father and former Pastor, Austin G. Mitchell and his beautiful wife, Cindy Mitchell, the Pastors of Via Dolorosa Gospel Tabernacle Church, located at 8300 Fenkell, Detroit MI. Thank you for all your prayers and support. God Bless you and The Via Dolorosa Church Family.

I want to thank my special friends that were there when I really needed Them, to Terri Perkins, Sylvia Rose, and Gail Witt, Peaches Lewis, just to name a few.

I want to thank each one of you for all your prayers, support and help that you provided to me in my times of struggles and hard times. Thank you for being there.

I want to thank my family members and friends for their prayers, support and open doors.

Published by: Xlibris
Edited by: Amanda Haddon(Niece) & Gail Witt(Write Image)
Copy Right 2007
Email: bencouragedlcm@yahoo.com & webbruthj@yahoo.com
Web Site: www.bencouragedlcm.org
Be Encouraged-Life Changing Ministries
PO Box 32114
Detroit, MI 48232

Opportunity

I would like to take this opportunity to introduce to you the King of kings, the Lord of lords, the knight in shining armor, the one that I know as my deliver, my healer, my provider; He is my redeemer my all and all. He is my personal savior. It is because of Him that I am alive today!

Nobody can ever do me like Him. He is awesome, He loves me like no one else can. His name is Jesus Christ.

Jesus loves everyone so very much. Whatever you've done, no matter the size or the incident, you can repent now and give your life to Jesus Christ and He will set you free from that bondage.

God will forgive you and he will never bring it up again. He remembers the sin no more.

The Word of God says, "For all have sinned and come short of the glory of God". We've all been there. We all had to repent and turn from evil to God! From our sinful nature to a living and loving God!

According to Romans 10:9, "That if thou shalt confess with thy mouth the Lord Jesus, and shalt believe in your thine heart that God hath raised him from the dead, thou shall be saved." If you believe and are ready, repeat this prayer to God.

> Father, in the name of Jesus, I come to you a sinner. I am sorry for all my sins. I repent now for every sin, sin I know and sin unknown. Forgive me and cleanse me and wash me with your blood. I give my life to you right now; be Lord and Savior of my life. I surrender my will to yours. In Jesus' name I pray. Amen

Beloved, heaven is rejoicing! If you prayed this prayer you are a born again child of God! You have given your life to the Lord Jesus Christ. I want to rejoice with you also, so please email or write me of this great news! God Bless you!

Chapter 1

Growing Up In the City

I often wondered what it would have been like to grow up in another city or country.

I used to imagine what it would have been like living in a mansion with maids and butlers to serve me. How wonderful it could be having all my financial needs met. It must be nice never having to want for anything.

I think about it, but I come to the conclusion that I would not have wanted it any other way. I can't imagine not having my mom Lillian Beatrice Mitchell, as my mother. Even though dad was very strict and hard on us, it was all for our own good.

I didn't like it nor did I understand it growing up as a child. But as I grew older I understood that it was beneficial for us. Because of Dad's firm enforcement, we learned how to have morals.

My mother, Lillian Beatrice Mitchell

My name is Ruth Janie Mitchell. My mother gave birth to my twin brother Robert and me on November 27, 1955. I was born 15 minutes before Robert, so that makes me the oldest. We are not identical. We were born and raised in the city of Detroit.

Form left to right: My dad(cut off), Uncle Neal center, end right, Cousin JC

My father, Benny Franklin Mitchell Sr., was a man that got what he wanted when he wanted it. He was the type of man who would blow someone's head off for disrespecting his family. I remember him pulling out a twenty-two rifle on two different occasions. When I saw that I said then, "My daddy will hurt somebody over us."

My mother, on the other hand was a whole different person. She was as gentle and kind as she could be. She was beautiful inside and out with a loveable spirit. I can't remember her ever yelling or getting loud with anyone; she was very soft spoken, always having something nice to say or a kind word that would uplift your spirit.

If mother didn't have anything good to say she wouldn't say a word.

Both my parents are deceased.

My father passed away when I was just eleven years old. It was in the fall of 1966, the month of September, on the 29th day.

My mother lost her first child. The doctors told her she would never be able to have any more children. Well, that was not true; Not only was mom able to have another child, but by the grace of God, she had six more children.

I am the third of six children born to this union. Benny Franklin, Jr. is the oldest, followed by Rose Laura, my twin brother Robert and me; Roy James, (who is deceased) and the last child, Kevin Ray.

I can remember when mom came home from the hospital with baby Kevin. We were all so excited! Dad and mom drove up; we were all looking out the window from the second floor flat with anticipation. Mom stepped out of the car holding a big blanket; a huge smile came on my face. We had a new baby coming to join us.

When mother got upstairs she laid the baby down and we all crowded around staring at the baby. Mother told us to get back. He was so handsome. He was almost as black as charcoal with jet-black wavy hair.

This all happened in the first house that I can remember us living in. It was on Glendale, in Detroit. We lived in a two family flat upstairs. My cousins lived downstairs. They owned the flat and dad was renting from them.

I can remember we had some bad days and good times in that house.

I don't like to dwell on the bad times, or the past, but it happened and I need to be able to talk about where I came from so that I can go forward. I prefer thinking and talking about those good times. That's life, I have to be able to take the bad with the good and be able to continue to live, love and forgive.

Holding on to the hurt and not forgiving will cause me to be bound by the one that hurt me. I won't have it. I am not bound; I am free! Thank God, I am free! Jesus Christ came that I might have life and that I might have it more abundantly.

As I reflect back on my childhood, it was there on Glendale that I remember my cousin JC and Uncle Neal putting their hands up my dress and rubbing on my vaginal area. I never said anything to anyone because I was afraid.

I was also in this house when I saw my dad drag my mother through the house. He would fight her, talk about her and put her down. I remember he pushed a very large dresser drawer on her. This was my first exposure to abusive men.

I regret that I never had the opportunity to know what real love was, until I met my husband Clarence. I regret never enjoying the pleasure of having my mother read me bedtime stories. Maybe mom never had books read to her; maybe she was just trying to survive the abusive relationship. I know that I am the cause of my children missing out on a lot. I couldn't be home with them. I was so distracted by my abusive husband that I didn't have time to do much of anything. I wish I could have done more with and for my children while they were young.

I often wondered what it would have been like to have my father accompany me to a father daughter's dinner dance.

I can't recall my parents ever telling me that they love me. As a result I found love in all the wrong places with all the wrong people. I just wanted to be loved and told I was loved.

Reflections

This is why it is so important to show children they are loved, and not only show them, but tell them. Teach them at home so they won't have to run to the first thing that says "I love you".

Parents, tell your children you love them. Tell them to dream big and dreams can come true. Don't put your children down or belittle them. Don't compare them to their mother or father; they are not mother or father!

Don't put one child over the other, always uplifting one child and putting the other one down. Never say, "You should be like your brother/ sister;" they're not them. They are who they are!

Learn how to award each child as an individual as well as collectively, but never one to the other.

Children need us while they are growing up to help lead and guide them in the right direction.

Don't tell them they shouldn't smoke when you smoke everyday.

Don't tell them not to drink when you do.

Don't tell them they shouldn't have sex until they get married when you have a man/woman spend the night with you every night.

Set examples and live by them.

I had to learn that you couldn't give what you've never been given unless God is in it.

God can and He will turn any upside down, messed up situation into victory. He will turn it around and make it work out for the good of them that love Him. What the enemy meant for evil, God will turn that thing around and make it work out in your behalf. I know I have been there when I didn't have anyone to turn to. I didn't know what to do. I called on the Name of Jesus and He turned my situation completely around. It was nobody but Jesus.

I know my parents loved me, even though they never told me. My dad was a great provider. He made sure all six of his children had food to eat, clothes on our backs and a roof over our head. I don't ever remember being hungry, not having clothes to wear or outside with nowhere to live. When you love someone you not only tell them, but you also show them. Put your money where my mouth is.

When I was a baby, I stayed in and out of the hospital. I had asthma and I was anemic.

Mom told me that I almost died. She told me that the doctors had to shave the top of my hair off so they could place tubes in my head. I thank God for healing me from both asthma and being anemic.

Today I don't have asthma nor am I anemic. God is truly a healer! With his stripes we are healed. KJV Isaiah 53:5

One time on Glendale, while we were outside playing, my brother Roy; his friend and I. I was about 8 years old. My little brother, Roy was about 5 years old. We were playing in the backyard.

While playing we saw a Faygo pop bottle with grape colored liquid in it. We ran over to the pop bottle. We thought we had found some soda pop. We just wanted something to quench our thirst.

I drank some, then Roy and his friend took a drink. The three of us took turns drinking what we thought was grape pop. Roy took the bottle and turned it up and didn't give it up.

Roy had drunk more than both of us. It was getting late so we went in the house and his friend went home.

Roy started acting very strangely. He started choking, so my parents rushed him to the hospital. As we entered the emergency room my dad said, "If that boy dies, I will kill you."

He was talking to me, because I was the one with him and I should have been watching him because I was the oldest. We found out later that the bottle really contained transmission fluid for an automobile.

After hearing my dad say what he did, I was so scared. I didn't know what to do but pray. My prayer was, "Please God, don't let my little brother die." I didn't know what caused me to pray at that young age, but I did and it worked.

The doctors came out from the emergency room where Roy was being treated. They told my parents that Roy had died on the operating table, but they were able to revive him and that he was in stable condition.

Glory to God! They think that they revived him, but I know for a fact it was the hand of God! God had answered an 8-year-old little girl's prayers.

That shows you that God is not a respecter of person. He just wants a pure heart.

If you can believe when you pray, you will receive. KJV Mark 11:24

The devil thought he had my little brother. God called out his name, "Roy" and told him to wake up, and his heart started pumping again! Thank you Jesus! God is a prayer answering God!

We moved from Glendale to Clements, off 14th Street. I can recall before the riot, in the early 60's, when we slept with our doors unlocked. We slept on the porch many hot summer nights. No one ever touched us. I won't do that today, times have really changed.

Some things just stick around in my mind and I just don't forget. During the era of the riot there were snipers on our roof. Somehow rioters got in our basement and were hanging out down there. I remember huge, green army tank trucks driving up and down my street; I watched them as they drove back and forth up our streets.

Burglars and thieves were everywhere. People were shoplifting food from grocery stores and stealing clothes from malls and even from the neighborhood cleaners.

We had just put our clothes in the cleaners the day before the riot broke out and we saw a man running down the street with our clothes in his hands, which he had stolen from the cleaners. It was a sight to see.

Stores and vacant buildings were being set on fire by arsonists, as the speeding fire trucks rode up and down the streets doing the best they could to put them out. I heard gunshots coming from the top of our roof. We had to lie down on the living room floor to avoid being shot by the stray bullets.

As I reminisce on my experience of living on Clements, I can recall being outside playing when all of a sudden the children that we were playing with started running to their homes. I asked, "Where are you going?" Everyone just ran I had no idea what was going on or why everyone was clearing the streets.

Someone shouted out,

"Run, it's the Auntie boys!"

I said, "The who?"

Robert and I were left outside alone with the Auntie boys. I didn't know what was going to happen next.

I had to see what was about to take place after seeing all my friends had run home to safety.

There were about four young boys in the gang. They all walked up to us and asked,

"Who are you?"

We told them our names and one of them said,

"Do you know who we are?"

"No!"

"Who are you, I asked?"

The leader told us who they were and told us what we were expected to do whenever they walked down the street. I let him know that I was not afraid of him and that I was not going to be running in the house when they came down the street. They got mad because I didn't run in the house when they came. They got revenge by breaking the flowerpots on our porch.

I don't know why I was being so tough, but I didn't let them make me run. I didn't fl inch. For some reason, I was not frightened of them and I never got beat up by any of them.

They lived on Grand, which was the street around the corner from us. They lived with their aunt. I was told that's how they got their gang nickname "The Auntie Boys".

One day they walked down the street and everyone ran except Robert, he was used to staying outside with me when they came down the street.

I heard some commotion outside, I ran to see what was going on. I looked out the door and they were pushing Robert and about to jump on him. I ran outside, "What's going on I said?"

"We're going to kick his butt."

I felt like I had to protect my twin brother. I said, "fight me instead." I was a tomboy. I liked playing with the boys more than with girls.

I was told, the leader of the gang liked me, and so maybe that's why they never messed with me. They stopped breaking our flowerpots too.

As I got older, I wanted to look like a girl. I had long, black hair and I couldn't do anything with it but put it in ponytails. I wanted to get my hair cut so I could wear some styles.

My older sister had gotten her hair cut and she could wear her hair in some really cool hairstyles. I begged my dad and he kept saying, "No, no, no." He said, "Ruth, if you get your hair cut you would want your hair back; you would start wearing wigs."

There was no such thing as weave at the time, if there was, I had not heard of it. I begged and begged and told him I wouldn't be wearing a wig.

I guess after all my nagging and begging I got on his nerves and he finally allowed me to get a haircut. My hair was sharp and very short. It kept growing back and I kept cutting it. Until after a while, it stopped growing back.

Dad was right; I started wearing wigs and weaves, paying hundreds of dollars for hair-hair that I once had for free, but cut off.

Then we moved again for the third time. We moved to Tuxedo. We were all known as the Mitchells. Our father had purchased a store. We sold candy, pop, chips, food, cigarettes, records, and much more.

He named the store Mitchell's Variety Store. It was located on 12th street off Richton, in Detroit.

We lived on Tuxedo. It was a big house. We had four large bedrooms. I really liked that house. I was so much smaller and the house seemed so much bigger than it was.

We were brought up staying to ourselves. We had to play with each other. We didn't have company come over and we couldn't go over to anyone's house. Dad did not let us spend the night and no one spent the night at our house. That's how I know that if dad had been alive as I got older, things would have been a lot different.

Dad would say, "They have a house, let them stay in it and you have one, stay in it."

He said my brothers and sister were my friends and that I didn't need any more than that.

On school nights I would have to be in the house before the streetlights came on. I got out of school at 3:00 and at 3:15 I had better be walking through that door of my house.

Dad told us that we didn't play on the way home from school; "Go to school and come straight home."

Many times I would find myself running home from school, out of breath, trying to make it home on time.

Other children would be playing and laughing, but not the Mitchells. We headed straight home after school.

When we complained to mom of his strict behavior, she would just say, "He loves you and wants you close to him."

Dad would work us! And we'd better not ask for any money. He would say, "I brought you into this world; that's your pay."

We all could have been doctors if we desired. He would have us rubbing and massaging him from head to toe.

He did not just use one of us, oh no, he would call all six of us at the same time. There we were, working on his body. One on his head, scratching it; one rubbing his chest and back in alcohol, two would be on the arms and hands, using the same alcohol and two on the legs and feet, passing the same alcohol.

I don't know if he just liked having his children close to him like mom said, or did he just want to work us because he could?

We would be downstairs playing, laughing and having fun then he would yell out to us from upstairs in his bedroom, "Clean up this house, now!" We all dropped whatever we were doing and we would immediately start searching for something to clean.

So, imagine this, six children walking around in their house, which was already spotless, trying to find something, anything dirty or out of order. What we would do was start asking the other one,

"Do you see anything?"

"Nope, do you?"

"Uhn, uhn."

So we all would just walk around looking like six zombies. I would start picking up lint, strings, whatever, just to be doing something and not get caught standing around, because if dad came downstairs and caught anyone of us standing around we would be in big trouble.

We had to sit at the dinner table all together as a family at dinnertime. It was not heard of to have one eating in his room and the other in their bedroom all over the house eating alone. No sir, we ate dinner together as a family. We had to eat everything on our plate.

I could not stand vegetables or bread and that was dinner one particular night. I ate everything else except the vegetables and bread. I asked to be excused. Mom said, "Sure." Dad said, "Not until you finish your dinner." I sat there playing with my food until it got late. I could hear my siblings playing and laughing, I wanted to go play. Everything in my plate had gotten cold; we didn't have microwaves back then.

I tried again to eat my vegetables and almost vomited. I started going to sleep on the table.

Dad had gone to sleep and mom came downstairs and told me I could get up. Mom was always the lifesaver.

Mother was a beautiful black woman. She had jet-black hair and as she got older her hair started to gray. She had this silver streak that started at the center of her forehead and went straight back. That streak of silver got fuller and fuller and her hair became salt and pepper, as she aged her entire head of hair was beautiful silver.

Mom was the sweetest woman I knew. I can't ever recall her screaming, cursing or yelling at us. I can't even remember her ever whipping us. I'd seen her angry, but it was the way she dealt with her anger that made a difference. She was kind and considerate to not just us, but to all those she came in contact with.

The Bible says, spare the rod spoil the child. When I was bad I expected to get whipped for it. But in my house we got beaten, what they would consider child abuse today. Anyone that grew up in my era knew about butt whippings and backhand slaps.

In my house if one of my siblings did something and didn't confess that they did it, we all would get a butt whipping so dad could make sure he got the right one.

We would have to line up outside the bathroom and once we got in the Bathroom, we would have to take off our clothes and get whipped naked.

The same line was formed when we had to take our medicine. We would line up outside the bathroom door and dad would be standing there with a spoon and the medicine. Once I got to the front of the line I would take it and go to bed or downstairs.

I remember one night my oldest brother Benny came in after his curfew. He knew he was in trouble. My dad didn't say a word, he went and got his twenty-two rifle, and cocked it. "Click, click."

Mother said, "Run Ben!"

He took off running, making for the front door. "Boom!" The loud sound rang out. Dad missed my brother, but he got the wall and there was a big hole to show that he was not playing. Dad would always say, "I brought you in this world and I will take you out."

Dad had us all afraid of him. His voice was strong and overpowering and his words were profound. He had that authoritative speech that got attention, never having to raise his voice or say anything twice.

God commands us to honor our parents and respect them; I should not be terrified of my father. Parents are not to provoke their children.

When we are afraid we can't express our true feelings. Why? Because when we are frightened of someone we're fearful of the consequences.

Chapter 2

The Old Homestead

In our house, during the late 60's, we had it hard. My dad did not play! He only had to speak once. He never repeated himself.

As I mentioned before, dad was very firm. He said what he meant and meant just what he said. He was good with the backhand slap across the face. My sister Rose got smacked in the face for wearing bangs. It was a style that girls wore, but not the Mitchell girls.

Dad would ask us all every now and then the big question? "What do you want to be when you grow up?" One would say,

"A doctor," another,

"A lawyer,"

I said,

"A teacher," my twin Robert, said,

"A cowboy."

Boy, what made that boy say that, is beyond me. We all saw the backhand coming. My dad slapped him so hard he flew across the living room floor.

I think Robert thought he was going to get praise when he said that, because my dad loved to watch cowboy movies, those old Western movies on the television.

I remember playing in the basement, kissing on my brothers, being mischievous and curious, as a young girl, playing house and acting like we were married. Touching and feeling in places that we as siblings shouldn't have and doing things we should not have been doing.

Reflections

Parents please give your children that so needed love and attention. The touch and feel of love is priceless. It is so necessary to say it as well as show it. That way they won't be searching for it in all the wrong places. Like I said earlier, I didn't know what real love was, so I fell for any man who said he loved me or had nice words to say to me. That's how a lot of our young ladies are being abused and misused, because they didn't get it at home so they're falling for the lies these no-good-for-nothing men tell them.

I can't remember being told I was pretty, I don't think my parents ever hugged me. Today, I am a hugger. I love people and I love to hug.

Don't get me wrong. There are still a lot of good God-fearing men out there. It just takes God to lead one to you.

One of the reasons a lot of our young ladies and young men are being abused, misused and disrespected is because they are not getting love at home, so they don't know how to treat a lady or a young man.

The mother is trying to raise these boys without a father and they can only do so much. Men raising their daughters, they don't know the different stages a woman's body goes through. They can be told and read about it but they can't experience it and so they can't explain it. That's why it takes a mother and a father to raise children. That's the way God designed it and it won't work out any other way.

I didn't say it couldn't be done. I know men and woman who have had to raise their boys and girls because of different circumstances and they turn out to be wonderful children.

Just because someone's father was an alcoholic doesn't mean their child will be an alcoholic. Things are passed down the bloodline. It is called the generational curse. This is where the sin of our forefathers have been passed down to the third and fourth generations. This curse can be broken. It's called breaking the generational curse. When you accept Jesus Christ as your personal savior you have the right to break the curse. KJV Exodus 20:5

When I found God, I found out that He loves me unconditionally, with no strings attached. He gives pure, clean and honest love.

I have learned that God is faithful. His Word will not come back to Him void or unaccomplished. He can't lie; He has no need to ever repent.

Before I knew God, I used all that as an excuse. Woe is me. No one loves me. Now that I have God as my Lord and Savior, I have the truth. After giving my life to God, I still have problems, but God has been with me every step of the way. I still had to go through many storms, and I still go through storms today, but He makes it easier to go through. I still face tests and trials, but my God orders my steps. Psalm 37:23

I see life under a whole different light. I see God working it all out for the good. I know God loves me! He has proven His love over and over again.

He didn't bring me this far to leave me.

Jesus Christ gave His life up so that we can live. That's love. Not only did He give His life, He was beaten beyond recognition! His clothes ripped off. Hairs pulled from His face! Spit upon, Thorns pushed down on His head and mocked!

He was whipped with hooks that literally pulled His flesh from His body every time it was snatched back. The whip was called cat of nine tails. All of this shame and pain and still He carried His cross down the Via Dolorosa road. He said no one took His life but He laid it down. Why? Because of love, He loves us so very much.

Why? For you and me, while we were yet sinners. What love! He died not because of anything that He had done, but for us. We were doomed we owned a payment. The payment was blood. He paid our debt. He knew no sin, yet He took the penalty of sin.

Just like Jesus carried His cross, we also have to carry our cross. There's a song out that simply says, "No Cross, no crown."

If we want to reign with Him we must suffer with Him. I have to carry my cross.

As a child growing up I had it hard. I thought that my dad was the meanest man alive.

I thought, how could God allow someone this evil to be born, and on top of that, have children to take advantage of. But really he wasn't that bad at all. He raised us the only way he knew how.

I remember my dad telling my sister and me that if either of us came home pregnant that he would kill us. I believed him.

I was in elementary school when he spoke those words to me.

This one morning was different than any other. There was this boy in my class who touched me on my butt, oh my goodness, how could he do such a terrible thing, I thought! I slapped him and said, "Boy, what are you doing? You're going to get me pregnant."

I was so unlearned. My dad didn't tell me how I could get pregnant, and I really didn't know. How can you possibly get pregnant from someone touching you? I honestly didn't know. The way that I learned about getting pregnant was in the streets, listening to people talk about it. I was never privileged to have the mother to daughter talk.

Reflections

Parents talk to your children. Let them know that you care. Tell them how much you love them. Tell them about the things going on today, so they won't find out the wrong way. I wish I had the opportunity to talk to my children more, I should have explained more, I could have done better; a lot of things I would've done differently, but you know it's too late for should-a, could-a, would-a.

Parents don't assume because you buy your child all the things they want and need that they know that you love them. It requires doing something, opening your mouth and saying it, "I love you." Open your arms and hug your children. Love is to be demonstrated; it is an action.

I was about eleven when I had my first period. I cried and cried because I thought I was pregnant. I told my sister; Rose and she explained to me that I had started my period.

I wasn't pregnant thank God! She explained that it was a normal female process. She told me how it works and what to expect. I was a bit young to be starting my menstrual cycle. Most girls didn't start until fifteen and older.

Tuxedo was a street to remember.

Chapter 3

Daddy is Gone

My dad worked at Chrysler and when he retired he drove a taxicab.

Dad had started to get very sick. He would cough up blood. He wasn't working anymore and he stayed in the bed most of the time. He was so sick. I remember him going from on-the-go daddy to staying-in-the-bed daddy.

He would rub holes in his t-shirts from rubbing his chest so frequently. We would still rub him down, but just not as much, because he didn't feel well.

I remember when we would be rubbing him down, I would hear the pastors preaching and the choir singing on the radio.

He had this silver servant bell that he would ring when he wanted one of us.

If he wanted one of us to get something for him, he would ring his bell.

We would all be downstairs playing and all of a sudden, "Ring, ding, a-ling" the bell would sound. We would be fussing about whose turn it was to go check on dad. One would say, "You go," another would say, "I just went now it's your turn." "I'll go next time." Back and forth we went on and on until the bell would rang out once again; then someone would shoot upstairs to check on daddy.

One afternoon I came home from school and cars were parked everywhere. I went in the house and there were people everywhere. They were standing around laughing and talking to each other. I had no clue of what was going on.

I had been to school for the entire day. Mom didn't come and take me out of class early. It was just another normal day, or so I thought, until I came home to see cars and people everywhere.

I was thinking to myself, what are all these people doing in my house? Why are all these people here? No one said anything to me; they just looked at me with this smirk like smile on their face. It wasn't a happy smile but it was a different smile. They continued to talk with each other.

Finally, mom came out of the kitchen; she came over to me and said your daddy died today.

My twin and I were eleven years old. Mother was left with six children to bring up on her own.

Daddy was gone. I was supposed to be crying or something, wasn't I? Shouldn't I have been feeling sad? After all, this was my daddy that had just died. I could not cry. I even tried to make tears come, but they just wouldn't come. Is there something wrong with me? I thought.

Reflections

How terrible I was, to be glad my dad had died. As I got older I asked God to forgive me, for the way I was feeling. When he died all I could think of was freedom! No more beatings. Now I can have friends, company in my house. I no longer had to run home from school. I am free from the mean old warden. This is what went through my mind after hearing those words come from my mother's lips. Daddy meant well. He wanted the best for us. Maybe he was never shown love, so he didn't know how to show it.

At the funeral I did manage to cry, after watching my mom and my siblings crying. I couldn't hold back the tears; they just flowed down my cheeks. They were real, but I can't honestly say they were because I was going to miss him. I think I was so happy and feeling sorry for mom and my brothers and sisters. For whatever reason, I know I had tears, why I had them, I could not tell you.

Dad had been gone now for about two weeks. I remember mom setting us all down telling us that we had to move. We were renting the house that we were living in. She said the lady who owned the house was putting us out because she had a family member that she was going to let move in. Isn't that something? Why didn't she put us out while dad was alive?

Mother went house hunting and found us a four family flat on Buena Vista, in Detroit.

So again we packed up our things and moved again, and we were renting. This time we didn't have dad with us. Benny, my oldest brother was the man of the house now.

We met new friends and stayed there for a while. Later we moved again. This time mom bought a house on LaSalle, in Detroit. She said that wouldn't happen again. When you rent you could easily be put out any time. When you owned, it belonged to you.

Mother tried to keep up the store that daddy bought, The Mitchell's Variety Store but we kept having break-ins and one night mom and my uncle were closing the store when some guy came into the store to rob them. He shot my uncle in the eye. He died. Mom hit the man over the head with the drawer from the cash register and the robber ran without taking anything. What a senseless crime and murder.

Mother's baby brother owned a distributing card company, and mom started working for him.

It was 1969, we were living in our new house on La Salle. We had a new birth, and a marriage, in the Mitchells family. Mom's first grandson was born and her oldest son got married. Benny and his beautiful bride got married in the backyard, and they live there today. They've been married a long time.

Chapter 4

A Young Teen On The Wild

I was a young teenager who was on the wild. My dad had passed away and mom was always at work, so I was on my own. I could basically do whatever I wanted to.

We had just moved to our new house that mom had purchased. I met some new friends. One acquaintance that I went to school with was jealous of me. Her boyfriend liked me and she thought I liked him. I did not. She always wanted to be the boss. If she couldn't have her way or if you didn't agree with what she would say or do then she would want to fight.

When I was growing up in the late 60's, early 70's, girls would fight you for their man. I could never understand that because I am not fighting over a boy, either he wants to be with me or not.

Robert got hooked up with the wrong crowd. The group he would hang out with would use drugs and drink alcohol. When I started going to high school I was offered drugs, cigarettes, beer and liquor. I tasted it, but it was nasty. I even tried the liquor and it burned my throat. The girls would say, "That's bold," "You're a square." These were words that we would say back then to indicate that you weren't hip or cool. I am so glad I had a bad experience with it all and I owe it all to God. The younger generation says words today that I have no idea what they're talking about.

Just because I was offered these bad things didn't mean I had to accept them. That's how Robert messed up his life, trying to be a part of the in crowd.

Everyone has been privileged to make choices. I choose to do sin (evil), or I choose to be obedient (good). I choose to destroy my body or choose to take care of it. If I'd chosen to take drugs, smoke and drink then I would have been destroying my body. Everyone has the same choice. What choices are you making?

If God Himself doesn't force us to do anything, no one else should either.

If you think that these things don't affect you and your body, you are absolutely wrong.

They do!

I wasn't sexually active. I would tease the young boys by wearing tight dresses and pants. I would wear lots and lots of make-up. I thought I looked good, my mom told me I had too much on, but I didn't listen I was young and having fun, and mom didn't know what she was talking about.

I would skip classes. I just didn't want to go to school. I didn't want to spend my day sitting up in some classroom. I had boyfriends; later they would break-up with me because I wouldn't have sex with them. I would let them hug me and kiss me, but sex was out of the question.

I wasn't ready for sex. Even though some of my girlfriends were sexually active, I wasn't. Boys would lie on me, by saying they had sex with me, but that was not true. I had a girlfriend that I thought was my friend. I would go over her house and often spent the night with her.

She lived around the corner from me. She would buy me things like candy or lunch at school. I would have dinner at her house. I thought that she was so nice and friendly.

One night when I spent the night with her she kissed me on the cheek. I didn't think anything of it, I just thought she was my best friend and that was cool.

So I kept spending the night with her and one night she kissed me on my cheek and then my lips. It felt good so I let her kiss me and I kissed her back. Then she got on top of me and started to roll on top of me. It felt good so I let her. I liked how she made me feel so I continued to go over to her house and we would kiss and lie on top of one another and roll until we would have an orgasm.

I wasn't expecting for this to happen, I just wanted a friend and she was there for me so I thought. Her intentions and motives were to do what she did. No telling how many young girls she turned out. How sad, because I didn't get the love and attention from home.

I never talked about it because I was ashamed and embarrassed. I told my sister-in-law what I had done as a young girl.

But in order for me to be free I have to talk about it, and so do you. Holding on to old past sin won't help. My saying is, "Tell on the devil."

I wasn't raised like that but I got hooked up with the wrong crowd, like my brother Robert. If my dad were alive he never would have allowed things like this to happen because we weren't able to spend the night out or have company.

I was young, foolish and unlearned. I was following my emotions. I did it because it felt good. It was wrong. I thank God that somebody was praying for me. It is the power of prayer that delivered me from that lifestyle.

My grandmother Rose Williams was my mother's mom. She was a praying woman. She would take us to church and vocation bible school. She loved God. I truly believe that she and the saints prayed for me.

Grandmother was just as sweet and kind as my mother was. I remember spending the entire summer at grandmother's house. She would buy us whatever we wanted.

I know for a fact that the effective prayer of a righteous person is powerful. When God answers prayers, situations have to change and line up with the Word of God.

KJV James 5:16 says, "Confess your faults one to another, and pray one for another, that ye may be healed. The effectual fervent prayer of a righteous man availeth much." I was too free and had no one to answer to. I could go and come whenever I wanted to since dad was not around anymore.

I wish that I had a mentor growing up.

Reflection

Too much freedom, no guidance, and no rules will cause some people to go in the wrong direction, if they got hooked up with the wrong crowd. Both my twin brother and I got deceived. Children experiment different things. That's why they need someone to lead them and help them make the correct decision.

I regret that I was the same with my children. I was not there for them. Everything else was more important at the time. I worked two jobs, went to school and left them home alone. I didn't have anyone around to say, "Raise your children don't let them raise themselves, and don't let them spend the night out." That is why I want to help someone, anyone, realize how important it is to be aware of your children's whereabouts at all times and whom they are with. Don't let them spend the night out, because anything could happen. I know it happened to me. Ask questions and do your research. Children go through different stages. Things like coloring their hair with all different types of colors, getting their body pierced, and dressing weird. Most of the time it is just a phase they are going through and hopefully it will pass. Don't be afraid to talk to your children; And don't just let anything and everything go on in your house. Parents have to draw the line somewhere.

I am so thankful that I discovered that I like men! A woman can't do a thing for me but be a friend. Listen and hear me good; a woman ain't got nothing on a man when it comes to having sex.

I know liking the same sex is a choice. It's a decision one makes. It is a lifestyle that one chooses.

I do not believe that men and women are born this way. It is sick and twisted. It is not the plan of God.

If God wanted the same sex to be together and have sexual interaction with each other, that is the way He would have designed us.

He would have formed from the dust of the ground, Adam and Edward or Eve and Edith. He gave men and women their sexual organs for a significant and specific use, to have intercourse and have children. Two men can't do that, nor two women.

When God created us He said, "Let us make man in our image and likeness." God is all man. God then from the dust of the ground formed He a male (man) and He then caused a deep sleep to come upon Adam and, created female (woman). There is nothing confusing about that. KJV Genesis 1:26

Anyone that is confused about his or her sexual status should seek God's face. Just like God delivered me, He will do the same for anyone that desires to be free. Allow God to cleanse you and make you a new creature.

There are those that are born with both female and male sex organs. They are called hermaphrodites. They also, have a choice to become male or female.

I was told that whichever sex is the most dominating that they would become that, be it male or female. The other sex organs would be taken out.

I have come to learn by experiment that everything that feels good doesn't mean it is good or that it is good for you.

We have a natural propensity for sin.

That's why we fall into sin, because it feels good to our old man, the flesh.

So we have sexual intercourse outside of marriage. We cheat on our spouse because we think the grass is greener on the other side. We smoke, drink, and get high because it feels good. All this is a trick from Satan. He is a deceiver. His intentions are to destroy our body, mind, soul and spirit. He sets us up and then makes us look foolish after we fall into his trap.

"Therefore if any man be in Christ, he is a new creature: old things are passed away; behold all things are become new." KJV 2 Corinthians 5:17 Whatever sin we partake in we must first confess it and then repent.

"If we confess our sin, He (God) is faithful and just to forgive us our sin and to cleanse us from all unrighteousness." KJV 1 John 1:9

No one can point the finger at anyone. Why? Because we have all sinned and come short of the glory of God. Sin is sin. There is no little sin or big sin. It all has the same price to pay. KJV Romans 3:23

All sinners will have their place in the lake of fire. If the truth be told, we have all done something that we are not pleased with or proud of. There are skeletons in closets that will never be let out.

The blood of Jesus Christ cleanses us; it makes us whiter than snow. Tell on the devil, regardless of how bad it seems. God can and will forgive you. Then he won't have anything on you. He won't be able to condemn you with that. What's done in the dark will come to the light. Your sin will find you out.

Reflections

Today, same sex relationships are so open, it is in our schools, in our churches. When they took prayer out of school then sin crept in.

Today if you speak against this terrible sin, you can be sent to jail. That just shows you where we are in life today. God hates sin. Just because down low, guys and lesbians have come out of the closet, doesn't make it right. I know God will forgive you and He will help you! It's the sin that God hates. That type of lifestyle is not normal. It is of Satan. The Bible talks about it being an abomination to Him.

Whatever it is that you are caught up in you can be set free. I couldn't talk to you about something I don't know anything about. But I have learned that God will allow us to go through many different things, so that we can help someone else. If I have been through it and God delivered me, He is not a respecter person, He will do the same thing for you. If you are hooked up in anything that goes against the will of God you can be set free, today! Don't be concerned about people, what they say or think. People will always have something to say. You might think you like it, but the devil has tricked you. He has deceived you.

You can pray right now to the Father, in Jesus name and watch God deliver you. But you have to want to be changed and set free. He will set you free from the hands of the enemy.

The Word of God says; don't fear those that can only destroy your body, but He who can destroy both body and soul.

Sin has a price tag. The wages of sin is death. Some things leave gradually when others leave instantly. You will still have tests and trials but the difference will be you'll have God to go through it with you. Like the story of the three Hebrew boys, they were tossed in the fiery furnace, which was heated seven times hotter than normal. God got in the fire with them. He'll do the same thing for us.

Those of you who are out there, you're confused; you think that's what you want to do. But you're looking over your shoulders, you can't rest, haven't slept in a long time, because you're sleeping with one eye open. Can you honestly say you are happy?

Chapter 5

My Experience With The Boys

One day my mother sent me to the corner store, King Cole's Grocery store. There was a light skinned young boy who kept staring at me and when I left the store and he followed me to the corner of La Salle. He stood on the corner of La Salle and watched me as I walked home.

He wanted to see where I lived. After I walked upon my front porch, I turned and looked down the street and he was standing there watching me. He was so cute, I thought.

The next time I went to the store, there he was again. This time he asked me what my name was. I said, "Ruth." He said, "My name is Terriono Del Terry Merriweather.

I thought he was teasing me. Who could possibly have such a name that long? Being as young as I was it seemed extra long for such a young boy.

I was thirteen years old when we met. Everyone called him by his nickname, which was Terry. He asked me to be his girlfriend. I said, "yes." We dated for three years. We would roll on each other but I was still a virgin when I broke up with him, so I thought. I've heard that rolling on someone is still a form of having sex.

Terry was my first, what you would call "puppy love." He was a very nice guy. He treated me with respect. I was too young to see that. I felt like he was too boring for me; I wanted some excitement. I went to Longfellow Jr. High School at the time.

Before Jr. High, I went to Custard Elementary School. That is where I met my best friend Zalena Slack. Her nickname was Toosie. We were friends from elementary until now. During Jr. High School she moved down South and we only talked when she came home to visit. She came back to Detroit after so many years and we still kept in contact. But our lifestyles are totally different.

When we were younger in Jr., High, Toosie and I were like sisters. She and I would skip school together over at each other's house. When we would skip, other friends and acquaintances would also come over. It would be about three and sometimes four couples skipping.

Sometimes it would just be the girls and no guys; most of them would drink, smoke, and have sex. Not me, I would skip class and that was the extent of it. If I had a boyfriend at that time we would kiss and I'd let him feel my breast, but that was the extent of it.

It wasn't an everyday thing; we would skip maybe twice a week. I would call the school and leave a message explaining why I would not be in school that day, each one of us did the same thing.

We all had colds, fevers, or some sickness that would cause us to be out for a few days. If the teacher called our house we would act like the parent because our parents worked. When teachers would send a letter home, our parents never got them.

It was the summer of 1973, when I was scheduled to graduate from Central High School. Had I been going to my classes like I was supposed to then I too would have been wearing a cap and gown. I thought I was being cool and getting away with something, when all the time, the joke was on me. I was the fool who missed out on a once in a lifetime experience.

Seeing my classmates graduated made me jealous. I wish that I had gone to class so I could have graduated. While I was skipping and having fun, my classmates were in class, studying and doing their homework. When graduation day came and all the things that led up to it, like the senior picnic, trip, pictures and the prom, I missed out on all that.

I can never get that back. I will never have the opportunity to do any of those things.

Education is so important. Get it while you can. It will pay off in the long run.

Let me take you back before I met Terry and started dating him.

I would date all the boys that no one else liked. I would feel sorry for them and date them just to make them feel good.

I would not let them kiss me. They could hug and that was the extent of it. I would let them say that I was their girlfriend because other girls would dog them out and make them feel like nothing.

I remember dating three boys at the same time. Well, they thought we were dating.

Whenever one of them would get too close and want to get serious, I would break up with him.

I was not trying to play any of them that was not my intention. I was helping them, or so I thought. I did not like any of them. I was trying to be a good person and make them feel good about themselves. But I was really hurting them all.

Not only was I hurting them, I was being dishonest. I never really acted like a girlfriend because they couldn't kiss me. I was trying to save the hurting world. What made me think that I, one young girl, could save the hurting and brokenhearted boys?

All I ever wanted was for them all to feel like they were attractive and that someone liked them, after hearing girls tease them about how ugly they were.

The way it all started was we would become buddies at school, just hanging out and going to parties together. They would for some reason feel they could talk to me. I would listen. I don't know if I was just someone they could relate to or if I was just ignored and tricked into feeling sorry for them.

I don't know what made me think I could make everything all better. They would tell me how some girl hurt their feelings and I would feel so sorry for them. So I, Miss save-the-day, Ruth to the rescue, would say, "I'll be your girlfriend."

I learned very quickly that I couldn't save the world. I can't keep people from getting hurt; that's just life. The majority of us will be hurt if we live long enough.

Well, that didn't last for too long. One hot summer evening they all decided that they would come over, all three of them. They had found out that I was not only dating one of them, but that I was dating all three of them at the same time. So they planned to set me up.

The three of them came over, knocked on my front door. I came outside and sat on the porch. We all went to the same school so you know what I did was extra stupid. It was foolish of me to think the next guy wouldn't find out.

I could imagine how it went down. One said,

"Yeah, my girlfriend is Ruth," and the other one said,

"So is mine," the other one saying,

"Ruth who?"

"Ruth Mitchell" they said.

I just imagine them talking to each other and saying she's my girlfriend and one saying she can't be, she told me she would be my girl, explaining how I look, to make sure it wasn't the same girl they were talking about.

So there we stood on my porch, all of us. One of them said,

"Which one of us is your boyfriend?"

Another one said,

"You can't be with all of us."

The third one said,

"So make your choice today."

I was silent for a moment, just because I didn't know how I was going to break it to them. Then I said,

"None of you."

Reflections

I felt so bad for what I had done. How I was no better than the girls that talked about them and put them down. How I hurt them even more because I lied to them. Trying to ease their pain from being hurt, I just made it worse.

They all walked off the porch. My mother's bedroom was right off the front porch. Her bedroom window was open; I hadn't really noticed it when I first went outside. But when I went in the house she said, "Ruth, you did the right thing."

I felt good knowing that my mother was listening, she heard it all, and I made the right decision.

After that I met Terry.

Chapter 6

Unwed Mother

I had a girlfriend named Carlene Roberson. Carla was here nickname. Carla was 6 feet tall and thick. I was 5' 3" and short and skinny. We became friends at Custard Elementary School.

I remember Carla would always bully me because she was so much bigger and taller. So while skipping school at my house, she and I got into a fistfight. I kicked her butt. She never bothered me again; we became best friends after that.

She is the one that introduced me to my first true love, Alfonzo. I broke up with Terry and started dating Alfonzo. He was the one who I gave in to and broke my virginity at the age of 17 years old.

I got pregnant while skipping school at my house on La Salle. I was seventeen years old not married, and having a baby.

Alfonzo asked me to marry him after finding out that I was having his child. He told me to ask my mother if we could get married.

I told him I asked and she said no, but I lied. I never asked her anything. Neither he nor I was ready to settle down and get married. We were both too young. I was not ready to be a wife or a mother, but I wasn't getting an abortion.

I was 18 years old when I had my son. On March 22, 1973, I gave birth to our child. We named him Alfonzo Drew Mitchell. He was my bundle of joy.

Alfonzo came early. I didn't go the full term of nine months. I was only eight months pregnant when I delivered him. Alfonzo weighted 3 pounds and 5 ounces. He was 18 inches long and born at General Hospital, in Highland Park.

His father and I broke up right after the baby was born. His parents Olivia and Roy, (who are both deceased), took good care of their grandson. I must say Alfonzo cared for his son. My baby didn't want for anything. He had food, milk, diapers, and clothes. Whatever Alfonzo Jr. needed, they would get it.

I was no longer with the baby's father, trying to raise a child alone. I had help with caring for his needs, but the staying up at nights and changing his diapers, feeding, doctor's appointments, dealing with the crying and getting up in the middle of the night was all on me. I didn't have any help in that department.

It was hard! I had Alfonzo's financial support, but the labor of raising a child was all on me. I continued to live with my mom, but she didn't help either, and she didn't have to. She had already raised her six children and did a great job doing it.

I was thankful that mom let me live in her house. Most parents were putting their daughters out if they got pregnant at a young age. I feel That's the time young unwed mothers' needed their parents to stick by their sides; Not to be talked about, or be pushed out on the streets trying to make it alone.

We had a roof over our head but I needed some finances to buy food for my son and me. I had to help mother pay the mortgage, utility bills and needed some money to pay for the medical bills.

I applied for Family Assistance, at the ADC office. I was approved for Medicaid, which paid for our doctor bills, food stamps, rent and utilities.

The experience of having a child woke me up quickly. It wasn't a game. I couldn't say, "I quit, and I'm going home." I had made my bed and now I had to sleep in it. I had to count up the cost, and the price wasn't pretty by a long shot.

I love my son, Alfonzo, and I will always love him. I just wish I had waited until I had got married before having a child, and that I would have graduated from high school.

I didn't have a life anymore. I couldn't just get up and go when I felt like it. Before Alfonzo was born, while I was pregnant, I tried to go back to school I was in the 11th grade, I didn't have long to go, but I just couldn't do it, I kept getting sick and I couldn't stay awake.

After Alfonzo was born, I tried again to go back to school to graduate, but Alfonzo would keep me up all night and I was too drained from waking up in the middle of the night to feed Alfonzo. It wasn't his fault; he didn't ask to be born, he was hungry and had to be fed.

It was my fault because I should have been in school. Isn't it funny, when I should have been in school, I wasn't, and now I wanted to go and I couldn't. I needed more sleep and I could not get enough sleep so I dropped out again.

My life now belonged to my child. He depended on me to raise him. He was my responsibility. I couldn't hang out with the girls like I was used to doing because now I had to try to find a baby-sitter, and they cost money. baby-sitter. So I would be stuck at home. My girlfriends would call and tell me how much fun they had and the guys that where there.

I was so young; my life was snatched away from me because of the wrong choices that I made. If I would have been in school studying with my head in my books and with my dress pulled down and legs closed it wouldn't have happened until I got married.

I am not saying my baby was a mistake. I love him, and I thank God for my son. But I was out of order; I was out of God's will.

God has ordained the way things should go. It is marriage first then children. Then you have help raising your children and you don't have to try to do it alone.

If I had my dad around, it would have been different. I would have been in school and not skipping. When daddy was alive, he made it perfectly clear not to come home with any babies. He would say, "Go to school and get your education and be somebody."

I was a baby myself having a baby. I had my whole life ahead of me to live and enjoy. But it was cut short. When I wanted to sleep, but couldn't because the baby wanted to play or eat. My eyes would be so heavy, I just wanted to sleep, but Alfonzo wanted to laugh, play, and be bounced. Many times I would just start crying because I felt so alone, and so young. Here I am a mother and I am only 18 years old.

I never blamed anyone because I couldn't; I did this to myself. No one forced me to skip or get pregnant. I just wish that I'd had a mentor around to help lead and guide me in the proper direction.

Alfonzo was my first priority making sure he was taken care of was now my first and foremost focus.

Reflections

I had dreams and hopes. My dream was that I would get married and have one husband, and we would have children together, not divorcing and having children out of wedlock. I had many dreams, but that dream didn't come true. I had three children who had two different fathers.

I have been married three times and divorced twice. Not my hopes and dreams at all. But that is life. If I would have done things differently, I could have possibly had my dreams come true.

Chapter 7

Baby Raising A Baby

**The first girl with the shorts and the vest on is me one
month pregnant with Alfonzo. My sister Rose is next to me.**

I was just a baby myself trying to raise a baby. With me being so young
I still wanted to go out and party. Even when I did get a baby-sitter and a
chance to go out, I was limited as to how long I could stay out!

I couldn't really enjoy myself because I was always thinking, is Alfonzo
alright? What is he doing now? I kept calling the sitter to see if he was okay.
I would leave early to get home with my baby. I guess that motherly instinct
just became a natural thing, the nurturing, caring love that mothers have.

Reflections

Young girls please don't be in a hurry to become a mom! It is not easy nor is it fun at all! Believe me, take it from someone that has been there and done it. Go to school and get your education and wait on your husband so you two can raise your family the way God had planned for it to be. It is a lot of hard work raising a child as a single parent.

Don't do it trying to keep a man; it is not worth it. If he loves you, and is going to be with you, he can wait until you get married before having children. Just because he says he loves you, don't give him the license to get you pregnant. Having a baby is the wrong reason to try to get a man to stay with you.

Alfonzo's father and I would date, break-up, date and break up. We would go back and forth, on and off. We had planned a couple's trip to Cedar Point with about 6 couples. Alfonzo had promised me that we would go; I was so excited and couldn't wait until that day came for our trip. When the day came for us to go, Alfonzo backed out. He said he didn't have any money and that we weren't going to go. Well, I knew that was a lie because Alfonzo always had money.

His mom, Olivia, knew how excited I was about the trip; all I did was talked about it. She gave him the money to take me. She kept our son for us. I was so happy!

I guess he was angry because he had other plans and his mom messed him up when she gave him the money. We rode with another couple. He started a fight with me as soon as we got in their car heading for Cedar Point.

He started telling me he had other girlfriends and that I didn't mean anything to him, how they were so much prettier and smarter than I was. He kept it up all the way to Ohio.

When we got to Cedar Point I went my way and he went his. I said, "That is it, we are finished." We drove home in two different cars. We never got back together after that. He and his family still took care of Alfonzo.

Alfonzo would come over or call, checking on his son asking me if he needed anything. I would tell him diapers, milk and food and he would bring cases of it over to my house.

I have to give a hand to Alfonzo; he was a great dad when it came to providing for his son, even though we weren't together. Most men just disappear after having a child and won't help out at all. This wasn't my case at all.

I was miserable. No fun, because I couldn't do the things I used to do. No life, because I had another life to be concerned about and my life meant nothing.

No friends, because they didn't have any children and they stopped coming around. When they did come around I couldn't talk to them because I had to keep my eyes and attention on my son.

When I was on ADC it was like abuse from the Social Workers, the long lines I had to stand in. The Social Worker would give me an appointment for 9:00 am in the morning and I had to be there and sign in. They would not call my name until 12:00 or sometimes even after lunch, and I would be there until 3:00, just sitting and waiting. Sometimes I would be in that office from the time they opened until the time they closed. That was ridiculous.

The things I had to deal with as a young teenager! Alfonzo would be crying, hungry and irritable (he and I both). Many times I left the ADC Office and wanted to cry. How could anyone make someone just sit for hours like that?

Then when they called my name, they would talk to me like I was dirt. They would tell me what I could and could not do or have. Things like, you can't work, and if you do you can only make so much. I couldn't have a car. I couldn't have a man living with me. If I did any of these things they would take me off.

Being so young, that seemed foolish to me. I thought how could I better myself if I didn't work? How could I get around if I didn't have transportation?

I was bound. I couldn't just get up and go, something I was so used to. Now if I wanted to go somewhere I had to bathe not only me but also my son. I had to comb my hair and my son's hair. Alfonzo had long braids so I had to braid his hair. Now when I was hungry I couldn't just fix me something right quick and eat, I had to fix my son something too.

There were times I was so hungry, since I had to wait until I fed Alfonzo first before I could eat.

Young, not knowing how to do some things and learning as I went, it was very hard. I would try to eat and feed him. But let me tell you, babies when they are hungry, they want to eat; you have to move fast. It seemed like as soon as I put a mouth full in and reached for mine he would start crying because I wasn't coming fast enough with the next spoonful.

I was so glad when he was able to hold his own bottle and feed himself. That was a huge help.

I became good friends with my baby's daddy's sister. We used to hang out tough. One holiday her father dropped us off at The State Fair, his sister, our girlfriend, and me. He drove us there but we had to catch the bus back.

Roy, my son's grandfather, was like a father to everyone. Every chance he got he would talk to me about "Those no good boys." Those were his words. It didn't matter where he had to take me, he would talk to me about boys, and school and bettering myself, from the time I got into his car until the time I got out. If I needed a ride anywhere, Roy would take me. He might fuss, but he would take me, fussing and talking all the way.

We had a great time at The State Fair. It started getting late so we walked to the bus stop to head home. We stood on Woodward at the bus stop, waiting for our bus.

While the three of us were standing there, these three boys came up to us. Each one of them chose one of us and started to talk.

William Collier III came over to me and started talking. We all ended up dating the guy that talked to us.

I didn't like him at all. He appeared to be too cool and slick for me. I should have followed my first mind.

He kept begging for my phone number so I gave it to him. He would call and I would have someone say I wasn't home. I didn't want to talk to him. He just kept calling and leaving messages. He would call and I would hang up on him. When I did talk to him he kept trying to set up a date with me and I kept saying how busy I was.

It was dark so I couldn't really see how he looked. I knew he had real good hair, black and wavy. I knew that he had a really big nose. I finally gave in after many refusals and hang-ups. I thought if I told him I had a baby that he would run from me, but he drew closer. We would just talk on the phone and he seemed interested in my son.

So we set a date, one of the biggest mistakes I ever made.

The girls dated but they broke up; I was the fool who married William. Why didn't I follow my first mind? I didn't like him for some reason. It took 15 long hard years of abuse and disrespect before I finally let it go. I am the type of person that when I say I am going to do something I try to do it. I try to be committed to my word. That's why I took so much.

Chapter 8

We Tied The Knot and The Abuse Started

He would not give up, so we started dating. He was interested in my son and I liked that. He would catch the bus to visit me on the West Side, and I would catch the bus to visit him on the East Side.

I would take my baby with me on the bus and William would catch the bus back to my house to see me home.

We were good friends. We would laugh and take pictures on the bus. He never showed any signs of being abusive. I enjoyed his company and he enjoyed being with me. He never hit me nor did he ever call me out of my name. He treated me with the utmost respect.

While we were dating I got pregnant. My son was two years old when I got pregnant I got an abortion. William cried because of my decision, but I was not ready for another child and I wasn't married. I told him I could not have another baby, especially since I was not married.

So we moved in together and we lived together for three years. One day I told William I'd had enough. I couldn't take it anymore. Playing husband and wife had come to an end. I wanted out. I gave him an ultimatum. I said, "We are getting married or I am leaving." I felt that three years was long enough to make a decision about settling down or moving on.

He told me he loved me but that he wasn't ready to get married. I told him that was fine and I moved out and got an apartment for my son and myself.

I found an apartment directly across the street from where I worked and around the corner from my mom. That worked out perfectly because some mornings I had to open up the cleaners. The day care was up the street from my job and my mother.

Everything was falling into place. I had determined within myself that I was not going to live with some man for the rest of my life and never get married and three years was the time limit. Whether he was ready or not, I had my time line set. He wasn't ready so it was time for me to move on.

I found out after leaving that I was pregnant. I told William that I was pregnant and that I couldn't keep it because I wasn't married. He said, "Please, don't get rid of my baby again. We will get married."

Because he said he would marry me, I kept it.

On July 27, 1975, I gave birth to a beautiful baby girl. We named her Kima Maria Collier. She weighted 4 pounds and 16 ounces. She was 17 inches long. She was born at Sinai Hospital in Detroit. She was my beautiful bald-headed baby girl; she had no hair at all on her head.

On June 30, 1976, we got married. We did not have a big wedding; we went to Toledo, Ohio and tied the knot. We lived in a studio apartment on the East Side. I was married now with two children.

My new name was, Ruth Janie Collier, I was so proud. Finally I was married to the man I loved and I thought loved me. We had it very hard trying to make ends meet and paying the bills. He started becoming very controlling and abusive.

I remember the first time he hit me. I had just cooked dinner and I was tired. He wanted some Kool-Aid to drink so he asked me to get it and I told him to get it himself, so he jumped up and hit me.

His hand went across my cheek. As I stood there in the kitchen, I didn't know how to take it. I didn't know how to react. The man that I thought loved me had just hit me. I felt distant and alone. I felt more hurt than the pain from the hit. I was hurt because the man I loved had just hit me as though I was the enemy. This was just the start of his excessive abusive behavior.

He started telling me where I could and couldn't go and who I could and couldn't be with.

In the midst of his controlling and abuse I got pregnant again. I was not about to have another baby with this abusive, controlling man. I was thinking about how I was going to leave him and a baby was the furthest thing from my mind.

I didn't tell him until after the abortion and I told him I was not going to bring another child into this world the way he was acting. He cried and begged me not to ever do that again. He told me he was under a lot of stress and that he was going to change. I believed him and agreed never to have another abortion again.

I was taking birth control pills, but I wasn't taking the pills regularly like I should have, and I got pregnant and I got my second abortion. I two abortions, one before my oldest daughter, Kima, and one after her.

I got pregnant once again that same year after the second abortion.

On August 16, 1977, I gave birth once again to a gorgeous baby girl. We named her Tisha Lena Collier. She weighted 5lbs and 14oz. She was 12 inches long. She was born at Detroit Medical Center.

Reflections

I had to learn that abortions are not the will of God. I felt so bad having the abortions that I had. I had to repent and ask God to forgive me, and He did. I am not proud of what I did. That is something I will never forget. I wish that I had never had any abortions. It was hard for me to deal with. I would think about it often and cry and wonder, what if they would have lived? How would they have looked? Who might they have been? I was tormented because of my wrong decisions. I will never know the answers to these questions nor will I ever forget. I know that God had forgiven me but I had to forgive myself. And with God's help I have.

Women, please, abortions are not the solution. God will provide for you to care for your baby. There are families that would love your baby and care for it. Abortion steals an innocent life. It is murder. Once it is done you can never undo it.

Please think about that innocent life. Think hard! It's a life that has every right to live, just as you and I.

I can talk to you about this and how it feels because I've been there and if I can help some girl or lady change her mind about having an abortion, my prayers will have been answered.

Chapter 9

The Abuse Continues

Maybe I rushed him into marrying me. I did give him an ultimatum and he did say he wasn't ready to get married. Here I was, nineteen with three babies who had two different fathers.

According to my dreams, I had it all planned out. The plan was supposed to be that in 1973 I would graduate from high school. Then I'd go to college for 3 or 4 years and then meet the man that God had ordained to be my husband, fall in love and get married then I'd find gainful employment or be the owner of our own business. We'd have babies and live happily ever after. Certainly no divorces or multiple fathers in the family. And absolutely no abuse.

That was my dream when I was a little girl, but I got sidetracked and that dream went down the drain.

Why didn't my dreams come true? Because I decided to settle for the first man that showed me love and acted like he cared. All the time it was simply a set up; it wasn't true love. I had to pay for it. Don't settle for less. You deserve the best. Just to say I was married, I settled twice. I could have done better had I waited.

If I had followed my heart and my dream I would not have this story to tell. I would have a story but a totally different one. It also would have been a best seller.

Reflections

Please, ladies I hope you don't fall for the first person that shows you some attention and tells you they love you, like I did. That's the problem, when women and men are being abused they always find a way to blame themselves for the abuse. That is a lie. It was not my fault my husbands were abusers, beating up on me. They both had issues. I did too because

I stood for it and stayed in those abusive relationships for 29 ½ years; 15 years with the first husband and 14 ½ years with the second husband.

Follow your heart; it won't lead you wrong. Follow your heart and not your feelings. Feelings will get you in a lot of trouble.

After that scene in the kitchen with him hitting me. I was shocked. I made his drink but I wanted to spit in it.

I didn't, but I wanted to. I was not going to let him make me like him. He apologized and said it won't happen again, but that was a lie.

He would get mad for no reason and start calling me out of my name. He would call me "stupid bitch", "lazy whore", anything that would put me down and make me feel like nothing. He would curse me out for no reason.

Then he would start throwing things at me, like the ash tray or whatever was near him. Then the slapping, name-calling and throwing things changed to fist fighting. He would hit me with his fist as though I was a man. I wouldn't fight back. He had a lot of anger inside that he had suppressed and then he finally let it out. He felt good when he would take his frustrations out on me.

I wanted to make my marriage work. I would leave and take the children and stay with my mother, until that got old. Mom wouldn't say anything but I knew it was getting on her nerves so I started going over to my brothers' or sister's house, until that got old too. Then I would take my babies to a shelter home.

I was a young mother, with three small children, married to a very evil, controlling abusive husband.

We moved from the studio apartment to a two family flat on Concord, off Mack, on the East Side of Detroit. We rented the upstairs flat. When I thought it couldn't get any worst, it did. He was so abusive, controlling and disrespectful.

One minute he would be nice and treat me so good. At times he would be so concerned as if he really cared. Then there were those days when I thought I was married to Satan himself. One night we were coming home after we had been out at the lounge disco dancing. It was William, his best friend Flip and his girlfriend, and me. All night at the club William danced with other women. I danced one time with another man and William was burning mad at me for that. I didn't understand how could he dance all night with other females and the second I get up on the dance floor to dance with another man I was disrespecting him. Well, if I was disrespecting him what was he doing to me?

I guess I was just allowed to sit there like a lump on a log and watch him dance and enjoy himself.

It was the last dance. The club was closing and he didn't ask me to Dance. He continued to dance with some girl. So a guy came over and said,

"Can I have this dance?"

I said, "Sure."

After that last song the lights in the club came on. He walked over to me and said something, but I couldn't hear him because they were making announcements over the microphone.

We rode in with his friend Flip; Flip drove his girlfriend's car, a brand new 1978 Concord she had just purchased. We argued back and forth all the way home sitting in the back seat of the car.

I was asking him how he could dance all night with other women and the one man that I danced with was a problem. I embarrassed him more than anything else.

When Flip pulled up to our flat on Concord, William hit me. I jumped out of the car and ran down the street. I got to the middle of the block before he caught me and when he did he started beating and choking me. He did that all the way back down to our flat.

He dragged me up the stairs still, hitting and beating on me. That was a terrible night, a night I will never forget.

Not only did I have to deal with the abuse from this man that kept telling me he was sorry and he wouldn't do it again, but the street was a nightmare. I would be sitting in the living room watching television and I would hear a loud bang. It was a gunshot. I would get up go look out of the window and I could see the neighbors shooting at each other. This went on all the time. I had to take my children to school in this neighborhood. I complained to my husband. I told him I couldn't take it anymore. I refused to take my children to school with all that shooting. So he bought us a house on Artesian on the West Side. Things were starting to look positive.

I now had a home that we owned, not rented. I had my three beautiful children and a husband who had a good job. That was most women's dream, to be married with children and own their own home. It was short lived.

The excitement from the new home had quickly faded away. William started back into his old routine again. He started staying out all night. The nights turned into two days, Turned into weeks. I was afraid to say anything. I just let him come and go as he pleased. I was glad when he was gone because I didn't have to deal with the abuse.

With his being away, he left me with the bills. Just because he wasn't home the mortgage, gas and lights still had to get paid. I went and applied for ADC again to help make ends meet. I was approved. They paid my mortgage, so much toward my gas and lights and I got food stamps.

I was married in name only, not as husband and wife. If something happened I couldn't get in touch with William, because I didn't know where to start calling. He wouldn't say, "If you need me you could reach me at this number."

He had me, (his wife), another family that he lived with and a girlfriend.

One day I remember my children telling me they were hungry. I looked in the cabinets and the cupboards; there was nothing. Not a thing to eat. My babies were telling me they were hungry and I didn't have any money. I had no idea where their dad was or even how to contact him.

I told them to set the table. I said, "We will eat today!" I had no idea where the food was going to come from, or how it was going to get on that table, but, I believed that there was a God!

And I really needed Him to come through for me that day to feed my babies. There was no one I could call to borrow money from to get food. The food stamps that I got monthly were already gone. I was borrowed out.

Alfonzo and Kima set the table. One put the dishes in place, the other one put the silverware in place and they both put the glasses on the table next to the plates. The youngest, Tisha was watching them as they prepared the table. As soon as they got done, I got down on my knees and began to talk to God. Before I could finish talking to God, There was a knock on the door.

I got up and ask, "Who is it?"

A voice answered, "Deacon Smith, from Greater Love Church."

I didn't know a Deacon Smith nor did I know anyone from Greater Love Church.

I opened the door. I saw men and women standing there holding bags, and bags and boxes and more bags of food! They said "The Lord sent us to your house." I never felt so good. God had answered my prayers while I was yet praying. I started crying and my babies were crying.

I told them that I was just on my knees praying for food because we didn't have anything to eat and I told them how I told my babies to set the table because we were going to eat today. Our faith moved God! Faith moves God.

God said if you can but believe he will bring it to pass.

I thanked them for being obedient to the voice of the Lord Jesus Christ. I asked them where their church was, and what time Sunday school started. They told me and I told them that we would be there Sunday morning.

They left and we were shouting and praising God. We began to put the food up in the cupboards, cabinets and refrigerator, which had been just empty but now held so much food.

After we put the food up I prepared a meal and we ate and ate and kept eating for days, weeks and even months from the food that they brought to our house.

Reflections

You can't tell me that God will not provide! I know He can! I know He will! God will supply your every need. No matter whatever it is, if you just have faith. I joined that same Church and not only did I join but I gave my life to God. That was December 23, 1983. I have been living for Jesus Christ and have not turned my back on Him. It is His grace and mercy that has kept us and brought us this far. He didn't bring us this far to leave us.

If you are struggling and it seems that you are in a trap and need to be set free, give it to Jesus Christ. He said, "Casting all your cares upon him; for he careth for you." 1 Peter 5:7

He promised that He would not put any more on you than you can bear. Sometimes it seems like we are in over our head, but God's Word is true and God cannot nor will not lie.

My word to you is, "Trust God all the way!" "His timing is not our timing." Wait on God."

Chapter 10

We Feared For Our Lives

My husband had all of us afraid of him; the beatings I took, and the whippings the children took. We were just there because we were frightened, not because we wanted to be there. I was too afraid to say anything to him and even more afraid of leaving.

He had threatened me. He told me if I ever left him he would kill himself, the children and me, and I believed him. He said, "If you ever leave me I will blow all of our heads off."

If I asked where he was, he would say something smart, like "None of your Business" or "Don't you worry about it. You just make sure you take care of the children and this house." He would be ready to fight me because I asked, as if I had no right asking him that question. After his tongue-lashings, I stopped even asking.

I wanted to leave him so badly but I was so scared that he would do what he said and we'd all be found in the house with our heads blown off.

I would say, "He's not going to kill us, he's crazy, but not that crazy." Then I would see him do some off-the-wall things and I would go right back into my shell.

He did things, like putting a rifle in my mouth and telling me he needed to just kill me because I didn't love him. He would blame me for messing around on him. He knocked my neighbor's front door in while looking for me because I had run over to her house to escape him, just to name a few of his off-the-wall mad behaviors.

He would come home and tell me about his other women; how he would have sex with them. I would be sitting up there listening to my husband tell me how he had sex with other women. Now you know he disrespected me. One woman he told me about, he said he was having sex with her and she had a bag for a stomach. How could he do that? Because the drugs he was using had taken over his mind, he couldn't have been in his right mind.

He would come home with other women's cars.

After dealing with William's abuse and the Social Workers' attitudes and their abuse, I got off ADC. I had it coming from every end. I could not take it any longer. I told my Social Worker that I no longer needed their services. I got my GED, started working two jobs and went to College. I was determined to make it without William and ADC. It was very hard working two full time jobs. I started at 9a.m. worked until 5p.m. then had to go straight to the other job from 6p.m. to 2a.m. Then I worked one full time job and one part time job so I could go to school. I majored in Accounting and Business. There were times when I had no transportation so I had to catch a bus to work and school.

Times were hard. So many days I went to school hungry with no money to buy any food. I would not give up. I continued to go to school and work. It took a toll on my body. The children were missing me and I was missing them, but I had to continue. I would have been better off without the extra weight of my husband.

My children never saw me because they were always with the baby-sitter. As they got a little older I would leave them home alone because I couldn't afford the baby-sitter. I would study and work, work and study day in and day out. I had to work very hard to keep the 4.0 grade point average that I had.

One day my husband came in and got all my books that I had paid for. He took all my papers, tests, and homework, every folder I had and tore them into pieces. He said I was going to school to find a boyfriend. He knew as well as I did that that was a lie! I was working two jobs and in school full time, how could I possibly have a boyfriend?

I had no time for a boyfriend, girlfriend or my children. When I got in for the night they were asleep. I would kiss them and do some studying before I turned in for the night. I was working and studying my life away. I had no life. Then he took all the torn pieces and burned them. After he did that he told me I had better not ever go back to school. I was so crushed. I could not believe he did that.

Now, all that I had worked so hard for was instantly burned and destroyed. The books I paid my hard earned money for were gone. All the studying, homework, test taking and staying up late nights seemed to be wasted. It had all gone down the drain. But, it wasn't wasted, it was knowledge that I had gained.

How could any human being be so evil, hateful and hideous? This was another one of his off-the-wall scenes.

When he destroyed my books and schoolwork it was in the middle of the summer term. It wasn't break or a holiday. He just wanted to be evil so he came in and did this dreadful thing. I begged him not to do that. He did it anyway. So he wouldn't feel so bad, he said I was cheating on him, that's why he had to do what he did.

All the time he was the one committing adultery. He was the one cheating on me. I never cheated on him; I was focusing on trying to raise my three children and extending my education.

It wasn't always that bad. There were a few good times, but the bad times out-weighed the good times by a long run. I remember one time I had decided I was leaving him, that was it, I could not take it any longer! I had it with the abuse, name-calling and disrespect. I went to my closet, took a few dresses and then went to the drawers and threw some things in a large green garbage bag. Then I went to the children's room and did the same thing. He came in while I was in the midst of putting the clothes in the bags. He asked me what I was doing.

I told him I couldn't take it anymore, that I was going to stay with my mom for a while. He was so nice all of a sudden. It was unbelievable. He helped me pack our clothes and then he said, "I'll take you over to your mom's house; it's the least I can do. I fell for that trick of his once again. Since we didn't have a car at the time, I was going to call someone to come and pick me up to take me over my mother's house. I had already called her so she was expecting me.

I had no idea why I would believe that foolishness. I guess I just wanted to get out and I didn't care anymore. As evil as he was, what would make me trust him? I said, "Okay!" He put our bags in the trunk and we all got in and left.

We got into his girlfriend's car, and we started towards my mom's house. We didn't talk at all. He didn't say a word, neither did I, nor did the children say one word, it was total silence.

We were on Evergreen. As we approached the over-bridge; he started speeding up, pushing his foot to the accelerator, all the way to the floor.

I said, "What are you doing?"

He said, "If I can't have you, no one else can have you."

He said, "I told you if you ever left me I would kill all of us, I can't live without you." He was quickly approaching the bridge.

I was in the front seat holding my youngest daughter, Tisha, my other two children, Alfonzo and Kima were in the back seat.

I didn't know what to do! Jump out of the car, is what came to my mind. Survival was the only thing on my mind. Before I could even think about it, I opened the door and jumped out!

I had Tisha; I knew he would stop the car if he didn't have me in it. It was me he wanted to kill, not the children or him. I was praying that he'd stop, because he had my other two children, Alfonzo and Kima with him. He stopped!

After I jumped out I thought about it. I said it was nothing but the grace of God that kept us protected from the on-coming traffic, which could have run us over. God had His angels encamped round about my children and me. God was truly with us!

I can't remember what happened after that. I just know he didn't kill us and I ended up going back with him. I was so hurt. I thought I was about to be free when all we did was go for a terrorizing ride with that crazy man who was my husband. I was so ready to leave and here I was, stuck in this evil, abusive, disrespectful house with this ludicrous man.

He was nice to us for one day and the second day he was back to his old self. It was hell that we lived in. I don't literally know how hell is, only what I read about it in the Bible and it sounds like a horrible place, a place I never want to go to.

That was the same feeling I had in that evil, despiteful and painful relationship called marriage.

God commanded the man to love his wife as he loves himself. How could a man love his wife and children and treat them the way that we were treated? It is impossible.

The hard times we went through were horrific. I can tell you about it, but you will never know what it was really like living it. After years of the put downs, being cursed out, beaten, cheated on, kicked, bitten and choked until there was no breath left in me; hit with his fist, a hammer, and a bat, not to mention the twenty-two rifle put in my mouth, I didn't know what to do.

He would curse me out because he just wanted to. He would beat me up because he was mad at his girlfriend.

He bit me twice. One night we were in the bed and he woke up and hit me. I got up and ran down the stairs. He caught me and took a bite out of my lower back. Another time he just got mad and grabbed my hand and bit the fat part of my lower thumb. I had to go to emergency and get rabies shots.

One night while we were asleep he just took his feet and kicked me out of the bed. He never had a reason. He would just do evil things. I never fought back; I just took it. But now he is paying for what he did to me.

I remember one of his girlfriends calling our house. She asked to speak to me.

I said, "This is she."

She said, "William told me to ask you if I can come and live with you two."

I could not believe my ears.

I said, "No!" and hung up. I asked him about it and he said she was lying. I knew she wasn't.

This same girl called my house again and told me she was pregnant. I told her to come over. She came over and was telling me about her and my husband's relationship. She said they had been dating for three years. I knew he had other women, but I didn't think he would try to bring his mess into our home. While we were sitting there talking, my husband came in. He had this shocked look on his face.

He said, "Come sit on this sofa."

We both did and he started cursing her out telling her she had no business coming over to his house. He went and got a hammer and started hitting her. I was in shock.

Then he turned to me and said,

"Why did you let her in?"

He started cursing me out and hitting me with the hammer. He left after that and I left and went to stay with my oldest brother, Benny, his wife and their children, around the corner.

I had to take off work because my head was swollen from the hammer. I could have died again; he hit us hard. He was trying to kill us. But God again stepped in and spared my life. The pregnant lady left. I heard she had a miscarriage.

I know it sounds unbelievable, but I went back to him again. That was the story of our marriage, back and forth, in and out.

He came in upset as usual and we got into it. I ran out of the house and he chased me down the street. He caught me and dragged me back to the front of our house. He started choking me. He choked me until I couldn't breathe anymore. I fell to the ground. He went into the house and left me there to die. God gave me breath again and I got up and went into the house.

My brother, Benny told me he saw my husband at the Festival Downtown. He said, "Your husband was wrapped up around some lady." He never took the kids or me out, he was too busy hanging out enjoying the single life.

When he came home I asked him about it. I said, "My brother Benny saw you today with your arms wrapped around some woman, I want to know who she was?" He started going off on me to switch the focus from him to me. I had given my life to God and I was not afraid of him anymore or what he could do to me.

So he started hitting me, and choking me and because I was so used to it, it didn't move me. I didn't cry like I used to. He went and got a bat and swung it at me. He tried to break my back with that bat. He hit me as hard as he could. I looked at him as if to say, "Is that all you got?" without ever opening my mouth. I then said, "No weapon formed against me shall prosper." I told him I didn't even feel it.

Chapter 11

Remembering the Pain & Hurt

Many times I felt like I had died and went to hell. Why me? Why was I going through so much pain and hurt? What did I do to deserve this type of treatment?

Would I ever be free from this? Whenever I left he would find me. If I went to a shelter he would call and say I know where you live. When I'd go stay with friends he would come over and tear up something at their house. It got to the point where nobody wanted me over because he would destroy their house by breaking a window or knocking a door down. My family tried to stay out of it. If my girlfriend picked me up he would follow us and run into her car. So there I was with no friends, and no family to turn too; just how he wanted it. I found out later that he knew women in all types of the work fields and that's how he got my information; they would tell him. He had a girlfriend that worked at the phone company, and she would give him any information he asked for. He was dating a woman at the Social Services Office and she would give him any information he asked for.

I remember one New Years Eve; we went out with his brothers and their wives and his sister and her husband. We had planned to spend this New Year's Eve together as family. Everyone was having fun, laughing and talking. Everyone, but me was drinking. I didn't drink. I knew how to enjoy myself without drinking and getting drunk. When the waiter came around to our table they would order their Rum and Coke, or whatever they were drinking and I would have a Coke or Sprite. I loved to dance.

My husband got drunk as usual and started dancing with other women. I had been sitting down for a long time, while he was up dancing with other ladies, song after song.

It was almost midnight. It was about to be a brand New Year! Everyone was dancing with his or her spouse or the date that they came with.

At midnight everyone was kissing his or her spouse and my husband was on the dance floor kissing another lady, in the mouth like she was his woman! He didn't even respect himself he did this in front of his family and me.

I said, "That is it!" I left the lounge. This is just a little taste of the disrespect I took. He did not have the decency enough to stop dancing with that other woman and come and give his wife a kiss. The way that he carried on with other women was no secret; he was open with his women, the disrespect and the abuse.

Roy, my brother had found the women of his dreams. They had dated for a while and decided to get married. His fiancée lived down the street from us on La Salle. Roy asked me if my two daughters, Kima and Tisha could be in his wedding as the flower girls. I was so excided; I said yes!

When I told William, he said no they couldn't be in it because we didn't have the money to buy both of them their flower girl dresses. I told Roy that they couldn't be in it because we couldn't afford to buy their dresses. He said, "No problem, I'll buy both their dresses.

That was just like Roy. He always helped me out. He was the one who always went to visit his siblings. He was so supportive. He would bring me bags of food and money because he knew that the man I had married was a loser.

Roy called me and said they were going to get the girls' dresses for the wedding. He asked me what size they wore.

I told him their sizes and he brought the dresses over later. The wedding colors were lime green and cream. I had them try their dresses on and they both looked like baby dolls.

The wedding day came and I had done the girls' hair and we all got dressed. I had a blue Pacer. We got in the car but the car wouldn't start. We went back in the house. My husband was in the house with his brother. He wasn't going to the wedding with us. I said, "My car won't start!" He acted as if it were nothing; he didn't say anything.

So I called my baby brother, Kevin. I asked him to pick us up. I told him I had to be there earlier because the girls were a part of the wedding party. He said, "No problem, I will be there in a minute."

When he got there he lifted the hood to the Pacer. He wanted to see why it wouldn't start. He said, "Someone took out your points and plugs." William had to have taken them out so we couldn't go; his scheme about us not having any money didn't work, so he took my plugs out.

Kevin came in after looking under the hood; he was waiting on me. William had called me upstairs. He was angry and wanted to fight. William started cursing at me and calling me out my name.

Kevin came upstairs and said, "What is going on? "I know you don't think you're going to beat my sister up with me here. Man what's wrong with you!" Kevin told him, "You are not going to beat her up with me here, come on Ruth, let's go."

William's brother, Thomas came upstairs to see what the commotion was.

After my brother said, "Let's go," I started walking down the stairs. William reached for me; Kevin grabbed him and beat his butt so badly! I guess he thought Kevin was joking, when he said, "You are not going to beat my sister up with me here." Maybe he thought because his brother was there they would double team Kevin.

All this chaos and I had a wedding to attend just hours away.

Thomas didn't do anything but look. After Kevin kicked his butt we left and went to the wedding. The girls did excellent in spite of the trauma. The wedding was beautiful.

Could you image what my little children where going through? This was a normal thing for them to see us fighting and arguing.

The time he pulled that rifle on me he was so drunk all he had to do was pull the trigger. I didn't go to sleep in the bed that night. I slept with one eye open on the sofa that was in our bedroom. With him being drunk I did not know what he was going to do.

I would go to the police station and file a complaint. I would talk to police officers and tell them what just happen and they would treat me as if I was the cause for what happened to me. One police officer said it had to be my fault. He asked me what I did to make him angry.

I had peace bonds on him. The peace bond would say that he could not come so many feet near me. He didn't care about a peace bond. He would tell me that it was nothing but a piece of paper and he was right. I would call the police and tell the officer that I have a peace bond on my husband and he is trying to get in my house.

They would say, "Is he in?" I would say, "No, that's why I am calling you." They have told me time after time, there was nothing they could do because he was my husband. I asked them why I should even get a peace bond if it doesn't work.

They would think I was getting smart and just say, "Mama it is nothing we can do unless he was in the premises. Maybe he knew someone on the police force because they were never a help to me.

So many women and men have died having a peace bond on the one that killed them. The police would always say they didn't get in domestic violence. This was back in the late 70's and early 80's. I think that they have gotten a little better.

William had gone out and bought two ceramic black bulldogs. You have to be careful with ceramic idols. You never know who owned them before you and what evil spirits had been involved with it. One morning my baby Tisha was sitting down in front of the television with her arm around one of the bulldogs, watching cartoons. I asked her, "What are you doing?" She said, "Me and my dog watching TV." She was about 5 years old and she said it just like that.

After he brought those dogs in my house he had begun acting like a dog. That's when he bit me twice.

I took those black bulldogs outside and threw them down hard on the cement ground outside, off my front porch. I was so shocked, what took place after that; I could not believe it, the bulldog did not crack or break. I said, "In the name of Jesus Christ!" And I threw it down again. That bulldog cracked and broke into many pieces; I did the other one too.

I remember we had this Ouija game board in our house. I don't know where it came from, but it was there in our house. I had played with it a few times. The object of the game was to find out your future. It had letters to spell out words. It had yes and no on it. I would put my two hands using my four fingers only on the game piece that would glide across the board spelling out the answer to whatever was asked.

I didn't know it then, but that was witchcraft. I was opening doors for evil spirits to come in. I did not need any more evil in my house. I took the game board and placed it in a garbage bag. Each street had a day that the trash would be picked up. When our trash pick up day came, I took the bag with the game board in it to the front of our house where the trash is picked up.

The trash men came and they took all the trash bags from in front of our house on the front lawn. Everything was gone. The next morning when I looked out the window I saw the Ouija board in front of my house on the lawn at the curb.

I did the same thing I did with the bulldogs. I used the name that is above every name. The name that has all power, so I said, "In the name of Jesus!"

I put it in the trash again and I never saw it again. Demons know the name of Jesus and they tremble.

Reflections

No one should have to go through the pain, hurt, abuse and disrespect that we go through as battered spouses or as people in battered relationships.

We are better than that. Why do we take it? Because we feel we can't do better. Because we have been put down for so long we have no self—esteem.

I am here to let every abused female or male know, that you can do better! You do not have to take the abuse. Take a stand and make a step out of that abusive relationship. With God, you can do it!

Divorce is not always the answer. Sometimes just separation will do. But stay separated until the abuser has been healed and delivered by God. God is the only thing that will change an abuser.

I had to seek help and still pray for total deliverance, because as an abused person I became an abuser. Not hitting, but not knowing how to say nice things. Not trusting anyone because I didn't want to be hurt again.

Not only did it affect me, but my children also.

Abuse affects more then the victim; it affects our children, family and friends. Like I always say, "God can and He will see you through, He will bring you out!"

Chapter 12

My Husband Goes To Jail

I remember William beating me up at our house. I ran across the street to Wendy's house, she was my friend and my neighbor. I ran and hid in her bedroom closet.

He ran across the street after me and broke her front door down. He came in looking for me. He went all over through her house looking for me, cursing me out. He told Wendy and her brother who was there also, not to get involved or he would blow their house up.

He couldn't find me so he left and went back across the street to our house. He called Wendy and said, "Tell Ruth if she don't get over here now, I will cut all these children's throats right now!" I was so scared I didn't know what to do. I told Wendy to call the police.

I stayed over at Wendy's until the police came. They talked to him and he told the police he would never do anything like that he just wanted his wife to come home. The police believed him. When I told them that he just busted my neighbors' door down, then they took him to jail. They only kept him for a few hours for questioning, then released him. He would always seem to talk his way out of jail. How could anyone just bust someone's door down and not feel anything?

I had left him. My mom was babysitting. She called me and told me that William had just come and took the children. He told her that he would bring them right back.

I knew how he was; I knew that he was up to no good. He came to my job and told me if I didn't come back to him that he would kill my babies.

He went and got them out of his car, they were glad to see me and I was so glad to see them. I hugged and kissed them and prayed over them. I told him that I would be back but that I needed some time to get myself together. I said, "Just don't hurt them."

I called his mother and asked her if she'd seen my babies. She said, "No."

My children told me later that they were there all the time at William's mother's house. They said they heard her tell me that they were not there. They said she was mean to them, that William would drop them off at her house and leave with another women. They told me that she would put them in the closet because they were crying because they wanted me.

Reflections

He would always use the babies to get me back. I would always go back because I feared what he would do.

You would think that had to be the end, right? Nope! There is still more.

I know that God had to be with my children and me. No human being could ever have taken this kind of horrific abuse and live, and not be in the mental institution. Except that God was with them. He was truly with us!

God can and will make a way of escape for you, just as he did for us, whatever it is. It may not be abuse, if you need to be free, all you have to do is call Him, Jesus is his Name. He has all power in His hand. He will deliver you.

I left him after 10 years of this back and forth, packing and leaving.

I had moved out of the house that he bought me on Artesian, which was on the West side. William would call me and check on the children and me. One day he called and said he had to go to court. I asked him for what. He told me that he had got into a fistfight with Flip. Flip was supposed to be his best friend. So I started asking questions. He told me that Flip left them at a party and that he and Thomas had jumped on him for leaving them without a ride home. I found out later at the trial that they beat Flip half to death.

We were seeing each other, but I did not live with him. We would talk and have sex; that was it. William called me and asked me if I would go to court with him to support him. He told me his court date and time. I don't know why; but I told him that I would be there to support him. What was I thinking? Support him, for what? After the way he had treated me and disrespected my children and me! He deserved just whatever he got.

Why? I can't tell you what caused me to stay and support him. Was it love? I don't think so. Was it fear? I think not. My chance to get out for good had finally come! But I just couldn't do it. I was addicted to him. I felt I owed him that much. Call it what you want, but I went. Really, I didn't owe this man a thing. I had been through ten years of hell. If anything, he owed me.

William and his brother were locked up in jail awaiting the trail. I still had the keys to my house on Artesian, so I went by there just to pick up some more of the children's clothes and mine.

As I walked through the front door there was this very eerie feeling as soon as I stepped in the house. It was a feeling of evil spirits lurking around. I felt as if someone was watching me. The house was dark, gloomy and cold. I stood there in the foyer for a minute. As you walk in the house there is the foyer; you could go left to the dinning room, which leads to the kitchen or right, which takes you into the living room. I went left into the dinning area. I tried to turn on some lights but the electricity had been turned off and there was no power.

I continued on towards the kitchen. I stopped before stepping into the kitchen and looked around. There was blood everywhere. I said, "Oh my God!" I looked down at the floor and there was a puddle of dried up blood all over the kitchen floor. The kitchen floor was covered in dried up blood. A floor that was once orange was now the color of dried up blood. Blood was on the walls, on the refrigerator; everywhere I looked, I saw blood. I stood there in shock! I thought, "That could have been my blood!" I didn't know what to do. I went and got a few things and left quickly.

I thought, "I have to go to this trial." I had to hear with my own ears what happen in that house that night. During the trial they talked about what had happened; how they beat him and beat him. How they hit him with different objects. They burned him with the hot iron.

When I saw Flip; he didn't look the same. They had disfigured his face. I felt so bad for him.

After the trial the judge set a court date for the sentencing.

I had called my sister Rose, and told her I had to go to court with William, and I asked her if I could wear one of her outfits to court.

I wanted to look good for William.

She said, "Sure." I went over to her house and went through her closet I picked out this royal blue after five formal. The dress came to my knee, and it had glitter on the jacket. Rose said, "Ruth, you don't want to wear that"

My sister tried to help me. Do you think I listened? No, not at all I was trying to look good for this no good man.

I went to court looking like a stone fool. I told her I wanted to look pretty, as if I couldn't be pretty with a regular outfit on. She tried to warn me.

I am sure everyone including the judge was all laughing at how foolish I looked. I was trying to help his case and instead I probably made it worse by looking like a prostitute. There I was in the courtroom at 9:00 am, with an evening dress on. I am sure everyone thought I was one of his hookers; I sure did look like one. I had the blue eye shadow on my eyes, red blush on my cheeks and heavy white lipstick on my lips. I looked just like a clown and didn't realize it, until afterward. I felt so silly and I looked ridiculous.

The jury found both of them, William and Thomas guilty of attempted murder. The judge sentenced William to 5 to 10 years in prison and Thomas got 3 to 5.

Can you believe I waited the entire five years for this fool? He was abusive and evil. He was an adulterer who told me about his relationships with other women, and who called me everything but a child of God.

He told me that he gave his life to God. Of course, I believed him. I had too; it was what I wanted for years. I was faithful to him for the entire five years while he was incarcerated. I would take my children up north to see him. He was moved all around during the course of the 5 years.

My three children and I would go up north and spend the night in a hotel and go see him the next day. I would drive us home after our morning visit. During the last of his five years they moved him way up North, past Mackinaw Island. It would take me 18 hours to drive up there and 18 hours back.

While he was in prison, I went back to school. So I worked two jobs and went to school full time. I wasn't getting the proper rest that I needed.

Chapter 13

It Was a Miracle

I was extra tired and I told William I wasn't going to be able to make it one weekend. I desperately needed some rest, which was well overdue. He kept begging me to please come because it was his baby girl's birthday. Tisha was turning 9 years old that weekend. I knew that I was too tired to drive the 18 hours there and back. The long hours at work and school and the long drive up north to see him had caught up with me. I told him no, I would bring her the next week; that I would be rested up. He just kept insisting that I bring her, so I pressed myself and drove down. We stayed in a cabin up north.

I made it a birthday party for Tisha. I invited my family. We had a picnic. My whole family came to visit William and sing happy birthday to Tisha. There was my oldest brother, Benny and his family, my oldest sister, Rose and her family, and my two younger bothers, Kevin and Roy and their families. We barbequed and brought all kinds of food. We even had a cake for her. It was the weekend of August 16th, Tisha's birthday. We had made it, we celebrated Tisha's birthday and were heading home. My oldest son, Alfonzo, was 13 and my oldest daughter, Kima, was 11.

It was August 17, 1986. My nephew asked if he could ride back with us. He wanted to be with my son Alfonzo. I said, "No, you ride with your dad." So we all said our goodbyes to William, and my family left. My children and I stayed for a few minutes after. It was time for everyone to leave and William prayed that we'd have a safe trip back home. We kissed, hugged and left.

I remember it raining and I had to stop at the gas station to get a fill up of gas to head back home. I knew that I was tired, but I didn't realize how tired I was. I remember getting gas and heading out on the road making it towards the highway. Everyone was tired and had gone to sleep.

I felt my eyes getting heavy so I let the window down. That didn't help so I turned up the radio really loud trying to stay awake. The rain was coming down and I thought I could make it to the next rest area so I continued to drive.

The next thing I remember was hearing the voice of God speaking to me. He said, "Take your knee out of the dashboard." I reached down and pulled my knee out. Then He said, "Unlock the door." I reached my hand up and unlocked the door. All the time I was out, everything seemed as if I was dreaming.

I began to hear voices of other people. "Are you alright?" The driver's door then opened. I was being pulled out of the car.

They began to ask me all types of questions.

Like, Miss, "where do you hurt?"

I said, "My nose, my eyes and my knee."

They asked, "What is your name?"

I said, "Ruth."

They asked me how old I was, I said, "thirty-one."

They asked, "How many children do you have?"

I said, "Three."

They then asked me. "How old are they?"

I said, "Thirteen, eleven and nine."

Someone asked, "What are your children's names?"

I said, "Alfonzo, Kima and Tisha.

I must have missed a few questions, because I heard someone say, "Ruth, Ruth . . . stay with us help is on the way!"

I tried to see what was going on, but I couldn't see out of my eyes. I could only hear voices.

I heard my son, Alfonzo, say, "Momma, why did you go to sleep?"

I said, "I didn't know I was that sleepy."

I remember writing with my finger, J E S U S, in the dirt on the ground. I started praying within myself to God. My prayer was, "Please God, don't let any of my children die!" "Lord, please do not allow anyone of us to die!" I tried to look around to see where my children were, but I couldn't see a thing. I kept writing in the dirt, J E S U S. I heard the EMS sirens as they pulled over to where I was. They took us all to a near by hospital.

I remember lying on a cold table for hours, it seemed. I was in so much pain. I wanted a doctor to come and get me off that hard, cold table and give me something for that pain. Finally, a doctor came in and said I had to be rushed to Ann Arbor University Hospital. They rolled me out past my children and I heard my daughter, Kima say, "Momma is going to die." I then heard Alfonzo say, "Shut up!" As I passed by them I said, "God is not going to let any of us die, God is with us and we are going to be alright!"

Alfonzo had a cut in his chin, which came from his jewelry he wore around his neck. He had a "D" made with diamonds his dad had bought him. His elbow was broken. Kima had a broken wrist. They treated Alfonzo and Kima by putting a cast on both of them and letting them go that same day. Tisha and I were hurt the worst. Tisha was asleep with her head on my lap in the front seat at the time of the accident. Tisha's hips were dislocated. Her legs were turned around backwards.

Tisha was in the hospital for a month.

William's mother stayed with her the whole time in the hospital that they had transferred her to.

When they took me to Ann Arbor University Hospital, they called my family in. The doctors told my family I wasn't going to make it because I had trauma to the head. I don't know if they left me on that cold hard table waiting for me to die. While on that table I was praising God all the time, thanking Him for life! My Pastors at that time, came up to see me, and they prayed for me. I could hear their voices but I couldn't open my eyes. All my family was standing around looking at me. I could hear them talking, but I couldn't respond. I was still lying on a stretcher; they had not taken me to a room. I was in so much pain.

Finally, after hours of being on that stretcher they moved me to a room. They removed all mirrors. They told me not to use any mirrors. I remember they let William out of jail (he had handcuffs on) to come up and see me because he was told that I was not going to live.

Doctors were coming in and out of my room examining me. There were interns and nurses also.

It was if I were on display. They would come with their pads and pens as they talked and wrote down what happened to me and what they thought about it and what they felt should be done.

The doctors told me my nose was broken. So they put a cast on my nose. My left jawbone was broken so I needed to have my mouth wired shut, with the tip of the wire coming out through the temple on my forehead.

Because both my nose and mouth were closed I had to have a tracheotomy tube (aid for breathing in a emergency) in my throat in order to breathe. The first time they had to clean it I thought I was going to die. I could not breathe. I did not like to get the tracheotomy tube cleaned because I couldn't breathe. My mouth was wired shut and my nose had a cast on it. Both openings were blocked. For a few seconds everyday I had to go through the experience not being able to breathe. They had to clean the tube everyday. My kneecap was busted open. My eye was hanging out. I had busted my tear duct. Also I had serious trauma to my head, which caused my head to become swollen to triple its normal size.

The doctors told me I was a miracle.

My family told me later as I began to heal that my head was the size of a basketball. They told me how the car looked. They said it was smashed in together from the front end to the back. The vehicle that I was driving looked like a squashed suitcase. I had fallen asleep and my car went across into the other on coming traffic. I hit a car head on, he was treated for minor bruises and released.

They told me the engine was in the front seat. The entire windshield was shattered. Glass from the windshield was everywhere. It was stuck in my face, and in my head. The accident was in the newspaper, which they gave me a copy of. It was also on the evening news. The brand new 1986 Alliance that God had just blessed me with was totaled.

They closed up my busted tear ducts. They fixed my eye, but my eye would run continuously. Tears would run down my face constantly from that one eye. They told me I needed to get another operation that would stop the tears from running down my face. I told them no. I said, "If God doesn't stop it from running it will run. As soon as I spoke that, the tears dried up immediately and straightaway. Just like that there were no more tears running down my face. God is truly a healer.

While I was in the hospital, I listened to church music and church services on the radio. I read my Bible and talked to God. They gave me morphine for the pain. Many days would pass and I would have no visitors. I felt so lonely and alone. I would pray, sing and thank God for life.

I was so happy whenever my family members, friends and co-workers came up to the hospital to see me. It was always a joy to have a visit.

I was in the hospital for over a month. The doctors and family members where so amazed at how God had healed me. I went to stay with my sister, Rose and her husband, Jessie. They were a huge help to me during this time. I thank God for them. I had lost so much weight because I could only sip liquids through a straw. I was already small, wearing a 5-6. I got down to a size 2 when I got out of the hospital. I may have been small, but I was alive! I had to learn how to eat again. I would walk like a mummy because I could not bend my right knee, the one that I pulled from the dashboard. Just think what would have happen if I had not listened to God and pulled my knee out of the dashboard. The people pulling me out could have torn my leg muscles. I had to go to therapy, but that didn't help, my knee still wouldn't bend.

When I went to the doctor for my check up, the doctor told me that he was going to have to cut off my leg because poison had set in and that it could spread even more.

I told him no. I said, "If God doesn't heal it, it won't get healed!" I said, "If God doesn't fix it, then I will walk like this for the rest of my life." I told them I was trusting God. Today, I have both my legs and God allowed me to walk a lot better than before. I know what God can do!

The doctors told my daughter Tisha that she would never walk again. When I got out of the hospital, Tisha was at my sister's house in a wheel chair. She had been in a body cast that went from her waist to her feet for about a month. When I saw her, I said, "Baby, you have to get up and walk, you can't stay in this wheel chair!" She told me what the doctors had told her that she would never walk again. I said, "We believe God!" I was not having my baby girl in a wheel chair for the rest of her life. God did not bring us this far to leave us alone. I never doubted God! Not once! I knew He was going to bring us all through it alive and He did just that! I said, "Baby, get up, you can do it!" She was afraid, but she got up. She tried and couldn't. I said, "Tisha, get up, you can do it. God is with you and I am right here. I said, "Today you will walk, in Jesus' name!" She got up again and took a step. It was hard for her, but she took another step, as if she were a new born baby learning how to walk all over again. Thank God she was walking again, something the doctors had told her she would not be able to do.

Today my baby is walking! We are all blessed and we owe it all to God! He spared all of our lives, and we will serve him!

This is our miracle!

Reflections

God is able and available for you; just call Him, He will answer you! He will deliver you! He will bring you out! God will be your strength, your joy, and your peace!

If you are tired of being sick and tired, of being abused, then cast all your cares upon Him, because He, (God) cares for you. I call Him Father, Daddy, Lord, and Savior. He is God alone, besides Him there is no other!

It's called relationship. If you don't have a relationship with Jesus Christ, you can have one. If you don't know Jesus Christ as your personal savior, you can call Him right now and He will save you. If you need help with the words to say go to the table of contents and find "Opportunity."

He is awesome! I would not be here today if it wasn't for him.

Another Miracle

If this accident wasn't bad enough, I had been diagnosed with cancer, over twenty years ago. I remember being in so much pain, I was hurting so badly that I couldn't stand up. I called my brother Roy, and he rushed me to the hospital.

The doctors told me I had cancer. I told them to let me get another doctor's opinion. They told me I didn't have time to get another opinion. So I prayed and let them do the surgery. People are dying everyday with the same type of cancer that I had. But the favor of God has been upon my life.

God is still doing miracles!

All my life the devil has been trying to still my life, but God has work for me to do.

The Brand New 1986 Alliance

I needed a reliable vehicle to get back and forth to work and school.

So, I had a little talk with Jesus. I remember reading in the Word of God, that I can have what I pray for if I believe. It read: "Whatsoever you ask, in prayer, believing, you shall have."

After my talk with God, not many days passed, when I had a dream or vision. I am not sure what it was, but I know it happened.

I saw myself in my baby brother, Kevin's car; he was taking me to pick up my brand new car.

In the vision, I was telling him how to get there.

So the next day I called Kevin and told him my vision. I told him I'd never been to this dealership, but I could tell him how to get there. He came over, I told him he had to get on the freeway and come up on Van Dyke. He said, "What's the name of the dealership?" I said, I don't know, I just know how to get there." So he took the freeway to Van Dyke exit and I said, "Turn left." He turned left and continued to drive down Van Dyke. I said, "I know what the salesman is going to ask me, and I know how I am to respond." Kevin kept driving. I said, "It will be on the left side on the corner." "Do you know the street corner, he asked?"

"Nope" I replied. As we approached this dealership, I said, "Get over. There it is!" He got over and turned up into the dealership Lot. It was a huge dealership; they had cars, cars and more cars. We got out of the car and headed inside to speak with a salesman. I saw the Alliance; it was so small and pretty. I said, "That's it!"

We went inside and a salesman came up to me and said, "Can I help you?"

I said, "Sure, I came to pick up a brand new Alliance, I saw it as I was coming in."

He said, "Alright, let's go take a look.

"How much are you working with?" The question I knew was coming. "I said, "One Thousand Dollars."

He said, "How's your credit?"

I didn't know that one was coming. I gave him my testimony. I said, "I had a dream about this car and this place and I'd never been here before. God showed me this dealership for a reason and I just came to pick up my new car."

I told him I wanted everything in it, sunroof, tape, leather seats. It was loaded, top of the line. He said, "We have to order your car if you want all that."

I said, "That's fine, when would it be ready?"

He told me it wouldn't take long that I could have it the next day. I said, "Alright, I will be here tomorrow to pick it up." I filled out the application, put the $1,000 dollars down and left.

I left the dealership smiling and thanking God for my new vehicle. I was about to have decent transportation.

Kevin dropped me off at home, I thanked him, and he said, "No problem."

I went to work the next day and at 2:45 p.m., my phone rang, "May I speak to Ruth Collier?"

"Yes, this is Ruth!"

"Mrs. Collier, we have bad news!"

I didn't say anything just listened. "Hello,"

"Yes, I m still here."

They continued, "Your credit isn't good enough to get the vehicle, I am sorry."

"Alright, thank you!" I hung the phone up; I was still excited, because I knew that God did not give me that vision for nothing. I was not losing my faith.

I went back to my work. The phone rang again. I looked up at the clock again. It was 3:00 straight up. I said, "Hello, this is Ruth."

"Mrs. Collier, I was calling back to tell you that you can come and pick up your car; it is ready."

I said, "Alright, thank you,"

I went to my boss and told her I had to go pick up my brand new 1986

Alliance. I called my mother and asked if she could come and pick me up to go get my new car. She said, "Yes, when?"

I said, "As soon as you get here."

She came and I went and got my brand new miracle that God gave me.

Reflections

God is awesome! Prayer is Powerful! When you pray, believe that God has done it and he will! It's not just about a car. It's really about having faith in God.

Having that relationship I was talking about earlier. What father doesn't want to see his child with the best? So much more does our Father in Heaven, want to see us with the finest things of this world. Beloved, I wish above all things that thou mayest prosper and be in health, even as thy soul prospereth. 3 John 2

Now, if He owns the cattle on the hills and the mansions, the land, the sea everything, why wouldn't he want his children to have a piece of it?

The Man at My Window Miracle

I was separated from my husband, William. I was living in an apartment downstairs from my baby brother, Kevin and his wife. My son's father, Alfonzo, had just taken my only son, Alfonso, away from me because of the threatened lifestyle I was living in. My son was eleven years old, the same age I was when my father died.

There were only my two girls, Kima, Tisha and me.

Kima was 8years old. She had gone over to her aunt's house to spend the night. So this night it was just Tisha and me at home.

It was late; we'd had a busy day, so we were getting ready to take our showers and go to bed. It was hot and muggy outside.

It was in the summer, one of those hot evenings in Detroit. It seemed as if there was no fresh air coming from anywhere.

Tisha was 6 years old. We would take baths and showers together sometimes. I got Tisha's and my gown out and put them on the bed and went to get into the shower. I stepped in the shower and I heard the voice of the Lord say, "Go to your window." I stepped out of the shower, grabbed a towel and walked to my bedroom window. I said, "What Lord, I don't see anything?"

"He said, "Look at your window." I notice that the window had been open much more than what I had opened it. "He said, "Go look out your window." I walked over to the window and there was a Caucasian man standing close up against the apartment brick wall. This white man had taken out my window screen and was about to come in. My brother lived upstairs, so I called him on the phone. I said, "Kevin, look out of your back window!"

He said, "What's going on?"

I said, "See that man?" "He took my screen out my window and was trying to come in."

Kevin said, "What!" "Let me get my gun." The man then took off running. I called the police, they came but nothing happen, and he was nowhere to be found. I shut all the windows, hot and all, and locked them and went to finish taking my shower. We said our prayers, I thanked God for sparing our lives once again, and we went to bed.

When we woke up the next morning, I heard the Lord's voice again. He said, "Go look out the window." I said, "Again Lord!"

I got up out of the bed and walked over to the window. I saw this large clear thick plastic body bag. I said, "Oh my God, he was going to kill us and put us in that bag."

Reflections

Once again God had stepped in and stayed the hand of death. The enemy wants us dead. He doesn't want us to serve and live for God. He's trying to take our lives before it's our time.

Having a relationship with The Father will make it much easier. What if I didn't know God? What if I didn't know how to talk to him and call upon Him? Then I would be lost, without hope! But I thank God that I do know Him and that I can call upon Him and He will answer prayer. Not only mine, but all of those who believe and trust Him. Sometimes we can't see our way through, but don't look at how to escape, don't look at your situation or circumstance, look at your Big God who can do anything. God has already promised to take us through. He has already said He'll never leave us alone.

No cross; no crown. Yes, the things we go through in life hurt, but remember, we're carrying our crosses. The tunnel seems dark and long, but just remember there is an opening at the other end of that tunnel. Just keep saying, "Daylight will come." It is right at your door. Don't turn around because you will have to travel down that same lonely tunnel all over again.

Just walk it on through and you will see that daylight was closer than you thought. Valleys seem low and mountains seem high. Remember there's no valley too low or mountain too high that God couldn't get you through.

Trust God! Never Doubt! I am a witness. He will see you through!

Chapter 14

The Last Straw

We all came through that ordeal by the healing hand of God. I waited faithfully for 5 years for this man that had told me he had been changed. He told me that he had accepted Jesus Christ into his life. So I believed him and waited. I just knew he was going to be a changed man. I knew he was going to treat me like a queen, after our lives were almost taken away, and after I waited for him faithfully 5 years, when he and I both knew he didn't deserve me; after driving 36 hours on weekends to go and visit with him for a few hours. I knew for sure that his love for me had to have grown stronger.

He still had control over my life even though he was locked up, behind bars. I had taken my income tax check and bought all new furniture and a brand new floor model television set for our home. It was so nice; the children loved it and so did I. He would call collect and I would accept the charges and he would send money home to pay the phone bill. I told him what I had done with my check and he told me to take it all back. He said we didn't need a new television or new furniture. I told the children I had to take everything back and they were so upset. I can remember Kima saying, "Why do you let him tell you what you can do? He's in jail." I was still being the good wife; I called the store and cancelled my order.

He never changed; he was just putting on a front. He still had other women coming to see him. He had women that took his conjugal visit with him, because I never took them. He finally got out after being incarcerated for five years. I was renting a house from my relatives. He got out and came to the house that I was renting from my aunt.

He had not been home for one week before he started up again with the same foolishness. He got drunk and laid on my daughter, Kima, kissing her in her mouth when I was at work. They were both fully dressed but that didn't change the fact that he was wrong. That was normal for him and his family to kiss each other in the mouth and feel on one another. There were six of them and it was the three boys that did that foolishness. Their dad did it, so I guess they thought it was the norm. He didn't have a job and he would lie around on the couch all day while I got up at 5 am to catch the bus so that I could get to work by 9:00 am, in Bloomfield Hills. He wouldn't even walk me to the bus stop until I said; "You could at least walk me to the bus stop." It was bad enough that he was there living off me, he had the nerve to bring his brother, Thomas in to lie around also. I was getting fed up, and approaching the last straw dealing with his foolishness. I told him that I wasn't putting up with the mess I put up with before. I told him if he wasn't in at a certain time the chain would be on the door.

One night he called; it was past the chain locking. I told him the chain was on and I wasn't getting up to let him in. He said, "If you don't let me in I will climb up to your window and break it." We had bars all around the downstairs part of the house, but there were no bars upstairs; it was a fire hazard to have bars all over the entire house. So he came and started banging on my front door, calling my name out loud, "Ruth, Ruth, come open this damn door."

It had to be about 2 in the morning. He continued to knock and curse. He said, "I'm coming upstairs and I 'am going to bust the window out." I got up, got the children and when he came up and was on the roof banging on the window upstairs I went to my neighbor's house and called the police. The police came and took him to jail. They only kept him until about 10 and released him. He called and said he was sorry he had too much to drink and that wouldn't happen again.

One day I went to work and had went to buy my lunch and my money was gone. So when I came home I asked him about my money; I never had problems with my daughters stealing from me. Now he's around and money comes up missing. All the five years while he was away I never had money missing. He got an attitude and said, "You need to check with the girls, they took your money."

Honestly I don't even remember how much it was. It wasn't much, $10 or $20; it was the fact that he came in and stole from me and to make matters worst, he blamed my daughters. He got mad because I believed my girls over him. So he hit me. I never fought back, but this time it was on. We were fighting. I was not about to go through the same mess all over again. I did not wait five years of my life for this. I had him in the headlock. I was kicking his butt. I said to my girls, "Call the police!" He threatened them and said, "If you touch that phone I will beat your butt". They were so scared they didn't call, they just sat there. He got loose from the headlock that I had him in and beat my butt. That was the last time he would ever abuse me again. That was the last time he kicked my butt. That was the last straw.

My daughters called me at work and said, "Momma, we are moving in with Christa and Kevin." That was my brother and his first wife. I went to work the next day and never went back. I never looked back. I left everything in the house. I only had the clothes on my back that I wore to work. I wish my children and me would have never had to be a part of this kind of abuse and control but it was in order to help someone else. If I had made a better choice in men, I wouldn't have had my son, my only son, taken away from me by his father.

The man was not home one week before I said, "This is the last straw." When you mean business about being free from abuse and control you will leave everything. Material things you can replace, but a life is irreplaceable. He called me at work the next day and asked me where I was. I told him we were gone and never coming back. He said, "You said you would never leave me." I didn't even answer him I was finished, I saw no need to go back and forth. He kept saying, "Can we talk?" I kept saying, "No, we have nothing to talk about." He started threatening me on my job, but it didn't work. I called the Police. They put a trace on my phone and they let him know if he called me one more time he was going back to jail.

He called, but stopped the threats. I would talk to him, but that was it. He couldn't believe it. It was hard even after all that, but I stood firm. I finally regained my self-esteem.

I didn't waste any time, I filed for my divorce after 15 years of that so-called marriage. I told the lawyer all the hell I had been through, how I had waited 5 years for him to get out of jail and that when he got out he started back doing the same thing after just one week. The lawyer got my divorce free of charge. I didn't have to pay one cent. Thank God I made it out alive and in my right mind. I was free!

Reflections

Follow your first mind; it is most likely to be the correct choice. Had I followed my first mind, I wouldn't have gone through this horrific pain and torture. How can anyone live with himself or herself after treating another human being so horribly?

I wasted 5 long years of my life waiting on him while he was doing time for a hideous crime. I gave him 15 years of my life and it was pure hell, I was terrified and miserable.

You've heard the old saying, "Three strikes and you're out." That's true for baseball, but when it comes to your life you're not playing a game. This is real, it's a matter of life and death and it doesn't take three strikes to get out!

I really thank God that I got out when I did, before it was too late!

Chapter 15

New Beginnings

I was free. I was waiting for my divorce to become final. I would no longer be Mrs. Ruth J. Collier. God released me from that controlling, overpowering and addictive spirit called abuse. After all the, "I won't do it again," and the "I am sorry." It was just words with no action or truth behind them.

While waiting for the divorce to be finalized, I took my daughters to a new church so that we could get a fresh start. While at our new church, my daughter, Kima noticed a man; he was big and tall in statue. She thought that he might be a good man for me. So she played matchmaker.

One afternoon after morning worship, she said to him, "Will you take my mother out to dinner?" He said, "Yes." We ended up at the church because of my friend, Precious. She was like a younger sister. God will place friends in your life, just at the right time; just when you really need a friend. I lived in Detroit and worked in Bloomfield Hills. I'd lived in the same house where I left everything behind, husband, clothes, furniture it all. No, I did not go back to him, this was before I left. Precious and I would ride the same bus to work; we worked at the same office in Bloomfield Hills.

I would wear high heels on the bus; I was so used to wearing high heels, that I really didn't pay any attention to it. It seemed normal for me to wear my heels on the bus and the walk from Woodward, which was about a mile to our place of employment. It was not unusual for me to walk a mile in my heels. I was used to it.

One day this young lady came up to me and said, "You should wear your gym shoes and walk in those instead of those high heels, it's not good to walk this long way in those high heels.

Precious was right, actually I never paid it any mind, because of all the other pain in my life, and I never really noticed it. I told her, "Thank you." From that day forward I never wore high heels to walk a mile to work again; I wore my gym shoes or flat shoes. I didn't realize how much pressure I was putting on my legs and my feet while walking in heels from the bus stop.

Precious and I became friends and have been friends every since that day. I am sure a lot of people were talking about me, saying how foolish it was to wear high heels and not low flat shoes. But no one ever said a word. I was glad she brought that to my attention. Those gym shoes felt so much better on my feet and it was better for my legs. God brought this friendship together through some high heel and gym shoes.

Precious, is a true friend. We don't have to be in each other's face every day, but we have that sister relationship. I call her mother; mom. Precious and I would go to Florida every year for our vacation. Florida is where her family is. Her mother is so sweet and kind, she reminds me so much of my natural mother. She always has a kind word to say; she loves Jesus Christ and will let you know it. She is always testifying of his goodness.

Chapter 16

I Married a Preacher

You would think after all I had been through in my 1st marriage that getting married was not on my agenda. I should have run in the other direction just hearing the word, until God had time to deal with me. Oh well, I couldn't just pass up this preacher, this man of God could I?

The only reason it wasn't sooner was because I had to wait until my divorce was final. We planned a big wedding for November 30, 1991. I had bridesmaids, groomsmen and the works.

Our family's tradition, each year, was to celebrate Christmas Eve at one of our homes, but our family had gotten so big with all the new born babies being added to the Mitchell's family, that we started to go outside of our homes so that all of us would fit. We would buy gifts, exchange gifts, play games and eat. We'd have a great time.

So I invited my fiancée, Kevin to the Christmas Eve Celebration.

My brother Roy was not feeling well at all. He was so quiet, and that was totally not Roy. Roy was usually the life of the gathering every year; he was the clown in the family, so he kept us laughing. He would say silly things and act silly, but not at this celebration. When Roy was there everyone knew that Roy was in the house. He had this funny kind of loud laugh that when you heard it alone, it would make you laugh. This time, something just wasn't right, Roy just wasn't the same. He was too quiet.

Roy had been feeling sick; he had gone to the doctor. I don't know if it was the medicine they gave him or what, but his feet were swollen up really big.

He pressed his way to be with the family for our family traditional celebration even though he wasn't feeling well at all. I had never ever seen Roy laid back and quiet. I was concerned. He just sat there in the chair quiet, not talking and in a lot of pain. It showed. This December 24, 1990 was not the same, Roy was just there. Roy said he couldn't take the pain much more.

So he had his wife gather their three boys, something Roy would normally do. We said our good byes, "Merry Christmas and we hope you feel better", and he and his family left and went home. Who would have known that would be the last time we would see Roy alive, that would be his last Christmas with the family? Christmas was Roy's favorite holiday, and the Lord took him home on that day. I wonder at times if Roy knew it was his time to leave us and that's why he pressed his way to see us for the last time?

On Christmas morning my son's grandmother, Olivia (who is deceased) came over, I opened the door and let her in, I didn't have a phone at that time and no one was able to contact me. She drove over; she lived around the corner from me. She said, "Ruth, your brother is dead." I said, "Who, Robert?" Robert was out there on drugs and doing some of everything, so I figured it was Robert. Not that I wanted it to be. I didn't want it to be any of my brothers. She said, "Roy." I dropped my head and started crying. I didn't realize he was that sick. I couldn't believe it; my little brother Roy was gone. Not Roy, he always helped me. I could always depend on Roy and he would be there for his big sister.

Roy was so caring and kind. He left behind three fine boys and a beautiful loving wife. Roy loved his wife and his boys. Everyone knew it. Before Roy passed, he came by my new house I bought in Oak Park. Roy said, "Ruth, be careful, I had a dream about you and it was in this house, I saw you get killed. That was Roy's first time coming to our new home. It wasn't my death Roy saw, he saw his own death. He saw death in a dream in that house but it wasn't my death.

I would be living in that house when he died. Not only did he see his death but our mothers also, and didn't know it. We had a family meeting at my house to discuss our next trip and what we were planning as a family for our next outing and upcoming events. Mother wasn't going to come, but she too pressed her way just as Roy did the night before he passed away.

Picture: Roy's wedding—Roy, his wife & my mother

She had stopped taking her medication a few months ago. She said she was tired of taking all those pills and she would lose her breath easily. Mother told me she wanted to take me Christmas shopping. I laughed and said, "Mom, it's only September."

She said, "I know, I want you to get whatever you want." She knew she was not going to be around by December 25th. Mother Passed away on December 2, 1993.

Mom was in a lot of pain, she never complained about the pain, but she would grunt all the time and she would always be rubbing on her legs in much pain. I didn't understand then, that mom knew she was leaving us too. She took about seven or more pills a day and she just got tired of the pain and pills. Mother was ready, she lived a long beautiful life, and she got to see her children grow up and some of her grandchildren and the most important thing was that she knew Jesus Christ as her personal Savior. She knew it was her time to leave this earthly vessel. She was going to be in a better place, a place with no more pain.

So I said, "I need a bed set."

She said, "I will take you to Art Van and let you pick out a bed and a mattress." She did, I picked her up and we went to Art Van on Greenfield and I picked out my bed and mattress.

After the meeting at my house everyone was leaving and there was a step missing as you walk down off my porch. Mom stepped down and almost fell. We were all talking, saying our byes when we should have been walking mother down those bad stairs.

Even though mom didn't fall, it knocked the wind out of her. If she had been taking her medication she might have made it. But like I said, mother was ready to go and she knew the maker. After mother got in the car she had a heart attack and Rose rushed her to Providence Hospital, which was right up the street from me.

Mom lived with Jessie and Rose, she had moved out of her house on La Salle and moved in with Rose so that they could be a help to each other. Mom helped Rose with her children and Rose and Jessie kept an eye on mom. Mother was in the hospital for weeks. I would go up there every day just about and talk to mother and pray, hoping to see some response, some reaction.

One day I went to see her and she didn't look the same. I said that day, "Bye mom, I can't come back up here and look at you like this." She was gone the day she fell; God gave us that time to be able to deal with it better; once we could say our good-byes, even though mother was with God the night she was rushed to the hospital.

Instead of just snatching mother away from us we were able to say our good-byes in our own way, during our time alone with her. We would go and pray and talk to her, we would say, "She moved her eyes," they kept telling us that it wasn't mom, that it was just her body reacting to the fluids. We finally all came to the reality that mother were gone.

All those fluids had mother swollen and disfigured. I refused to go to the hospital again and see my mother like that, I said, mom is with the Lord, this is just a body that she used while here on earth.

The doctors called us all together and said we had to make a decision what we wanted to do with mom.

So her baby brother Ray (who is deceased) and all five of her children came together and met at the hospital and the majority of us said take her off the breathing tube but Kevin my baby brother didn't want to. But we let him know that mom was gone, she was with God now. That was a sad time.

If you lost anyone close to you, you know how it hurts. Even though you're a born again child of God, it hurts because that special love one is gone and you won't be able to talk to them any more, laugh with them any more.

We all have to go one day when God calls our name. Hopefully we will be ready to meet Him.

We told Kevin that God don't make mistakes, God knows what's best.

It would be selfish to keep mom here. So we all agreed. It was so hard, but it was the right thing to do. Mom was gone. It was just an empty body blowing up from all those fluids being pushed into her.

It's a hard thing but it makes it a lot easier when you know that your love one loved God and knew God as their personal savior.

Being engaged to Mr. Kevin Ray Simmons was not so easy. It was weird that they both had the same first and middle name. My brother is Kevin Ray Mitchell.

I had to put up with some really foolish stuff with my new fiancée Kevin.

One evening he picked me up from work and he asked me what I wanted to eat. I told him I didn't care that it really didn't matter. He said, "You don't know?" His whole entire attitude and demeanor changed. He said, "The wedding is off!" Just like that. I could not believe it that he would call off the wedding because I said it didn't matter what or where we ate.

That is just a tastes of what I had to deal with.

Anyone with any kind of brains would know that no one calls off a wedding because of something like that; something else was going on with that picture he had other issues.

He took me straight home and dropped me off at home I didn't see him or hear from him for weeks. What it really was, that he was with some other woman and he used that as his excuse.

I know, I should have called off the wedding and never spoken to him again because he obviously was sick. That was my sign to get out and run as fast as I could and never look back. This man was sick!

That was my sign but did I listen? No! I was even sicker to continue the relationship with him. I brushed it off and I made some excuse for his odd behavior. Anytime men or women just go off for no reason, don't believe it's nothing, they start a fight to get free for awhile. Everyone knows that old trick. After two or three weeks he made some excuse and we were back talking again. I thought, "He just had a bad day." If that wasn't stupid enough, like I said, what it really was is that he wanted to be with his other women.

I can't honestly tell you how many times the wedding date had been called off and cancelled by him before we actually really got married. I am talking about a man that calls himself a pastor and a preacher, a man of God acting and behaving in this manner. What was wrong with me? Was I desperate for pain? Did I need a man that badly that I would settle again? Did I really enjoy the abuse? I didn't think so; I was used to being hurt and it seemed normal to me. It's sad to say, but it is the truth. Women who are abused for so long get addicted to it. Not that you want it but it is something that becomes the norm for you. Just like any addiction.

I should never have rushed into another relationship, especially getting remarried. I should have taken that time to get Ruth together. Ruth needed so much healing and help alone. I fell right into the enemies' trap. I felt, because he had said he was a man of the cloth and he preached God's Word, that he couldn't be half as bad as my first husband. Oh was I wrong, this man was the worst! It was like going from the frying pan to the fire.

While dating him I would let him stay over and I would always say, "We can't do anything until we get married." But this one night he took advantage of me and he raped me. It was rape because I was not in agreement with what he did. I was so surprised, hurt and shocked that this so called "man of God" who said he loved me, would do such a thing.

He was preaching and teaching the Word of God and so was I, but we were not living it. We were in sin, fornicating. Here I was, asking God to forgive me, and I continued to do the same thing all over again. That wasn't repentance; that was remorse. I had to tell him he could not spend the night anymore. It takes God to give you the strength to be strong and you can be if you listen to the voice of God. I was so strict, but he would say things like, "I am going to be your husband, its ok." I knew that it wasn't ok, but I wanted to please him. How foolish was I? I felt violated. I should have called the wedding off for sure after that. But again I made excuses for his inappropriate behavior and I forgave him.

Reflections

Words of Wisdom, when dating, even if you're engaged to be married, keep a chaperone around. Never say what you won't do, the flesh is weak.

Never find yourself alone in a quiet place with someone you love because the devil will start speaking to you. Keep friends around. Go on dates where there are lots of people and then go home. Never let them spend the night. You don't have to test the product.

If you're engaged, move the date up. The Bible talks about if you're burning, you should marry. Sex before marriage is not God's plan. 2 Corinthians 7:9 "But if they cannot contain, let them marry: for it is better to marry than to burn."

I had all types of signs that this was not to be my husband, but like a lot of lonely men and women, we just simply ignore the signs. Kevin could be so kind and caring at times and the next minute he would snap and be as evil and mean as the devil himself. One night I got a phone call. It was very early in the morning, about 2 am. My voice mail picked up the call. This strange, weird eerie voice said, "Hello." The sound of the voice alone was evil and something about it seemed demonic. The ring woke me up, but I didn't feel like getting up to answer it. I let the voice mail answer it. Just from the call alone I felt this eerie feeling. I said, "I will check it out in the morning." I fell back to sleep. They didn't leave a message, the voice only said, "Hello, Hello." But it was scary; the voice didn't seem like a human being's voice.

I asked Kima if she heard it and she said yes. Kima and I were the only two that heard it, Tisha didn't hear anything. I said "It sounded really strange." Kima said, "Yes it was your friend Kevin," I said, "No, it was Larry." (her boyfriend at that time, who is now her husband) Since we couldn't detect who it was, I said, "Let's listen to the call, it came on the voice mail."

So I rewound the message and pushed play and it was blank; nothing was on the tape. Nothing was on the tape. I said, "What happened?" I felt it was an evil spirit when I heard it. It had to be, because nothing was on the phone. So I asked Kevin and she asked Larry, they both said it wasn't them. My question was how could I even hear a voice say hello if the machine wasn't on. When the voice mail picked up I clearly heard that scary voice say hello. I am convinced that it was some evil spirit. Satan is a spirit and he can't operate without a body or an object. We weren't dreaming because we both heard it.

One of the preachers from the church came up to me and said, "Kevin doesn't love you; he just wants your money. But I really didn't have any money so I didn't believe it. I did find out later that he was a con-artist.

God will bless you and make it appear as though you have lots of money, when you really don't. When I told Kevin I didn't have any food he would help out, buy food, and help me with my bills. On our wedding day, Kevin came over to my house. He knocked on the door. I was getting ready for the wedding that was at 3:00 that day. I asked him why he came over. He didn't even say hello, he acted very strange for someone who loved me and was about to marry me. He said, "I lost my money and I need $500. He knew I had it because it was to pay the final payments towards the wedding. We still had to pay the preacher and for the rental of the church. He said, "It's an emergency, if it wasn't I wouldn't be asking you." I was a fool in love and trying to help him out, I went to the bedroom and got the money and gave it to him. I asked him, "What were we going to do about paying the preacher and for the Church?" He said he would take care of it. I fell for that con-artist on my wedding day. I really didn't think anything of it. I had so much more on my mind. It was my wedding day. All of that planning time involved and today was the big day.

My wedding day, I should have been so happy; everything was done and ready to go, all I had to do now was walk down the aisle and say, "I do." But I was concerned and worried; all I could think of was what could be such an emergency that he needed $500? I was so upset because I gave him $500 and I didn't know why. Here we are about to start our lives together as husband and wife and he can't tell me the emergency. He said, "I don't want you to be worrying." But how could I not be? I wanted to know what just happened to my $500. I still didn't put two and two together.

He just kept telling me not to worry, but common sense would've told me that we should be able to share and talk about anything; pain, sorrow, joy and especially money. I later found out what the emergency was. Why he didn't want to worry or concern me. He told me himself that on our wedding day he went and bought his baby's momma a car with my money that I had given him; No he didn't, use my money, I was going to use on my wedding! He had the nerve to buy his ex a car with my money.

He planned that, just so he would be able to throw it up in both our faces at the opportune time. I found out when we were in a heated argument. He said, "Remember that emergency on our wedding day?" I bought my baby's mother a car, with your money.

I wanted to choke him. But my life is more precious to me than he is. I didn't want to spend the rest of my life in jail for a silly mistake.

He did it, I am sure, to get on her good side by saying, "I don't love her, I bought you a car with her money." This is a man who says he is a preacher/pastor.

That was so wrong. Yes it did hurt. But the Word of God tells me that you will reap whatsoever you sow. When you sow to the flesh you will reap corruption. That is God's set rule.

Galatians 6:8

Reflections

Women & men, please listen! Don't let your significant other spend the night, ever. You say with your mouth what you will and will not do, but the flesh has other plans. The flesh is weak. It takes a strong man or women of God to leave when it gets too hot. Kissing and "touchy-feely" will get you in a lot of trouble. Take it from someone who has been there and done it.

When I thought I was strong, I was weak. I truly love God and I am a firm believer in God's Word, and I slipped, I would never have if I had a strong man thinking the same way I was, which was let us wait until we say "I do".

The devil is busy, but my God is even busier! God gave us power over the flesh, but we have to use it. Just because we have that power doesn't mean it is going to do the work for you. Rebuke the devil, we have to do something first. After we rebuke him, he will flee. Satan is not going to just leave. Don't play with or tempt the devil, do what the Word commands us to do.

James 4:7 Submit yourselves therefore to God. Resist the devil, and he will flee from you.

God was trying so many times to get my attention, but I was not hearing Him; I wasn't listening. He was trying to show me all during the relationship, even on my wedding day, but I wouldn't listen. I was going to make it work. I should have said, "I've got it and you ain't getting it." Especially if he can't tell me what the money is for. I was blinded by what I thought was love, but it was really just lust. I was determined I was going to be married and it was going to be right this time, even if I had to do it myself. Well, you see I couldn't do a thing, if God isn't in it, it isn't going to work. Hear me. I can't change anyone and if God doesn't do it, believe me, it won't get done. The person has to want to change because God won't and doesn't force anything on anyone. You've heard the saying, "It takes two." Well, I am here to tell you, "It takes three, God, you and your spouse." God must be included in everything, every step of the way. Not some things or some times, but everything all the time. Don't wait until things get rough and hard and then you invite God to join you. That's okay, but it is even better when you can include him everyday, every step that you take. God will lead and guide you into all truth.

While we were dating Kevin told me over and over again, that if our marriage didn't work he was going to get a divorce. He entered our marriage with the wrong motives. Why go into a marriage talking about divorce? Divorce should never be an option. This was another sign that I let get by me. Every disagreement or argument that we had, his famous words were, "I will get a divorce." After we got married, it was, "I am getting a divorce." I can't tell you how many times he spoke those words to me before and after our marriage. We were married for 14 ½ years, and I honestly can't tell you that we stayed together for one full year without him leaving me or me leaving him. Why? Because he had a plan, that plan was to get a divorce. While he was working hard to end the marriage, I was working hard on keeping the marriage together.

Reflections

Ladies and Gentlemen, my brothers and sisters, if your fiancée/fiancé tells you that they will leave you if it doesn't work, RUN!!! Run because he/she is going in with the wrong attitude, intentions and wrong motive. When you marry someone it should be forever, until death do you part; that's God's plan. No one gets married planning on his or her divorce, that's ridiculous.

Marriage should be forever, that's how God ordained it to be. Your love should be unconditional. What if God would have loved us conditionally? We would all be lost and without hope.

Marriage is a vow made before God, between two people. God said, "If you make a vow (promise), you should not take it back, it is better not to make a vow (promise), then to make one and take it back. Ecclesiastes 5:5

God said that if you lack wisdom all you have to do is ask. He will teach you how to be a husband, how to treat your wife. How you are to love and cherish her. How you should build her up and not put her down. How you should encourage her and not belittle her.

Learn how to speak positive things and not negative. Learn how to say your wife is a virtuous woman, even if she isn't. If you say it enough, it would happen; words have power.

Allow God to teach you men how to be the man of the house. Take your rightful place in your household and stand up and be a man.

You heard me say, "I was going to make it work." I can't make anyone do anything, neither can you. The person first has to recognize that there is a problem, that's step number one. Then they have to acknowledge that there is a need for a change in them.

A person that won't be changed is one that blames everyone else but himself or herself. Everyone else is wrong by them. It is always the other person. They never did anything; it's always the other person, if you let them tell it. That's a soul that won't be delivered or healed.

All relationships have some type of problems, because we are two different people and we think differently, we were raised differently. But you have to work on it, learn how to respect the other person. Know that you are not right all the time. You can't get your way all the time. Be willing to give and take. Be honest and open

Don't ever enter a relationship thinking that you are going to change that Person. I have a News update report: you will not, nor can not change others.

Don't think once you tie the knot, all will be fine. That is a lie straight from hell. Marriage takes work, hard work. Why? You will have to learn each other. Dating and living with someone is totally two different colors.

A lot of times what we do is marry for the wrong reasons, and love is nowhere in it. Sex, money, appearance, freedom and so many more wrong reasons are why we say, "I do," when we really don't.

All those things are nice: A good love maker, you meet that special someone that knows how to make you feel so great, someone that has it really going on in the finance department, that person whose beauty turns heads every time. And what about the looks, when the shape and muscles changes from a coke bottle to a huge ball, or a huge ball, to a stick, those muscles disappear. When that which attracted you leaves, what then? Do you leave too? I sure hope not. Make sure you're getting married for the right reason.

Sex is great; God designed it for married couples to enjoy. Wait until you get married. God said, for better or worse, richer or poorer until death do you part. Not until we see a finer sister/brother that's paid. No, until death do we part? That means to stand through it all. Marriage is precious, and special; and it is should be; God ordained marriage.

Chapter 17

The Preacher is Cheating

My daughter Kima would turn her music on and listen to the tapes and he would get up out of bed in the middle of the night, get dressed and say nothing. I asked him, "Where are you going?" He said, "I am leaving, that music is too loud." I tell you the honest truth. He would not get up and go tell her to turn the music down or just turn it down himself, like any normal man would do. He could have said, "Ruth the music is too loud; can you have her turn it down?" I would've had no problem with that. The music didn't bother me, I was used to them playing their music I could sleep with the music going; evidently he couldn't or he had other plans.

This man would leave and be gone for weeks without calling or coming home. If that isn't a sign of cheating, what is it? It became so obvious that he was cheating. He would get mad and leave and come back when he wanted to.

He would not touch me for months. We would walk through the house not talking to each other for weeks at a time, and what makes it so bad, we were both preachers. He would say, "You're so dumb, you should know I am getting it (sex) from somewhere, I haven't touched you." My reply would always be, "God will deal with you." Yes, it hurts when your spouse confesses to you that he is messing around on you. All I could do was pray and ask God for strength and direction. Know, I am asking God for direction, when I should have asked before I got married. But I didn't want to hear God then, I wanted my flesh to be satisfied. So I settled for less and I paid for it.

One Sunday morning while we were in church, he said, "I am not coming back with you tonight to night service. I thought that was strange for him to mention that during service; why couldn't he tell me after morning worship, on the way home? He said it again; as if he had to make it plain; "I won't be coming to night service so don't ask." After we got outside, I asked him, "Why did you keep telling me that?, I heard you the first time you said it?"

He said he didn't want me asking him because he was tired and he was staying at home. Our home was Candle Woods Suites, a hotel where we were paying $450 a week. I will explain this story later.

We would go to church and after church go out to dinner and get home and take a nap before it was time for evening service.

We did the norm, while we were asleep, his pager went off. It was on vibrate so it woke me up. He didn't hear it. I got up and checked his message. It was a woman. She said, "Hi honey, are you still coming tonight to my service?" I woke him up, I said, "Your girlfriend just called, she wanted to know if you were still coming tonight?" "That's why you kept telling me you weren't going to night service, because you already had plans to go, but not with me." He denied it, of course. He said, "That lady had the wrong number." I wasn't falling for that, I packed my clothes and moved it with my son. I stayed with him for about 3 weeks before I got back with Kevin. My children could not stand him. The children could see right through him. Where I was blinded by what I though was love, they saw straight through him.

We moved so many times, I can't remember how many. When we first got married, he moved into my house that I owned in Oak Park. Kima, Tisha and Alfonzo had sued my insurance company from the accident we had. The girls used most of their money for the down payment on the house we purchased in Oak Park and I paid the house note each month. The house was $35,000 and they put down $25,000. I asked Alfonzo if he would give us the remaining amount to pay the house off in full. He said, "No." He was not giving up any of his money. Because they were too young to collect, they had an overseer, like a lawyer, to protect their money. When they turned 18 years old they received their money.

He couldn't get along with Kima; they seemed to hate each other. Both said they were born again Christians. God is love; where was the love? It would irritate him when the children would knock on the door when we were in the bedroom with the door shut. They would knock on the door to ask me a question, and sometimes just to get on his nerves. Because they kept saying that it was their house we were living in he finally said, we're moving out of their house; let them have their house. I kept putting it off, because I couldn't leave them at that young age. They would do things to upset him and he would leave and come back. One day they did something that really made him mad He said, "That's it; let them stay in this house we can move to an apartment."

Kima is the tallest and oldest and Tisha is the shorter and youngest. Kima is a designer and she designed the dress she is wearing.

We are talking about my two younger daughters, Kima and Tisha that he's asking me to leave in the house. Kima was only sixteen and Tisha was only fourteen. They both were too young to be on their own. How could I? How could I allow this no good man talk me into leaving my daughters, to whom I gave birth? Evil spirits blinded me. As I look back, I would not have ever done something like that being in my right mind. What I thought was right was wrong. I asked Tisha to come with us and she couldn't leave her sister; I am glad they stuck together. The time they really needed me, I walked out on them; I have prayed and asked God to forgive me and I have asked their forgiveness. I cried many nights, in pain and hurting for leaving them. I was wrong to leave my girls. They were my responsibility. If no one else cared about them, I should have. They were children, so they acted in such a matter. But it was not a cause to leave them in that house alone. That was not a good move, but I was trying to keep peace in the house. I didn't know what else to do. I wish I had not moved.

I feel like his plan was to destroy my relationship with my daughters. A real man or women of God would have put their rules out and stuck by them, not run away from the problem, but deal with it and pray about it. Seek God's face for direction. Kima had it so hard trying to keep up the house. It seemed like everything got turned off. She got behind in the bills so the lights, the gas and the water were shut off. When I heard about everything being shut off I was so hurt. I tried to help but he wouldn't let me. He said, "She's grown, let her take care of herself." I was trying to be a good wife and obey my husband. He was really out to destroy our relationship. That was evil. God at times would soften his heart and make him give me money to buy them food.

He had no friends and he wasn't with his daughters so his plan was to destroy everything I had. He didn't want me to have any friends. He felt I was too close to my children.

But God provided for my babies. He brought them out and God is still providing for them. I wasn't there like I should have been, but my prayers were with them.

I made so many mistakes. I was always trying to hold on to good-for-nothing men. I thought that they loved me, when it was my children who really loved me all the time.

It was their father: the abuse I went through I didn't go through it alone, they went through the pain, hurt, torture and embarrassment just as I did.

Then I brought this man who I really didn't know, into their lives; a man who was claiming to be a preacher but who was a devil in disguise. How could any man of God allow such a thing? God is love! But, we reap what we sow.

Reflections

God said He would fight our battles. He told us He would not put any more on us than we can handle. He said He will never leave us nor will He forsake us.

God is true to His Word. He can't lie, neither is there a need for Him to repent.

Whatever situations life deals your way; know that God is a God that will deliver you out of the hand of the enemy. I am a witness.

Sometimes we can't reach our loved ones', for some reason we can't get to them. We can't be there for them, But God is available 24/7: twenty-four hours a day and seven days a week.

We can call on the Father, in the Name of Jesus and He will answer prayer. I am a living witness that prayer changes situations. In spite of our shortcomings, in spite of our faults, we have a mediator whom we can call upon. Repent of our sinful ways and watch God move on your behave.

He will work out that situation that seemed impossible. He will create a door where there was no door.

He might not come when you think He should, but believe me, He is never late!

There was an incident that took place before we moved out of the house.

Kima's girlfriend, Marsha, came over. After we told her she couldn't come In, she came in anyway because Kima said it was her house.

There was a big fight. We ended up in the bedroom. Kevin went into the kitchen and got a knife; I grabbed Marsha and was lying on the bed holding her down.

My husband and Marsha were arguing. I did not want anyone to get cut.

The police came and we tried to explain that we asked Marsha to leave and she would not leave; she ignored our request and she came in anyway.

Kevin had a very bad temper. I told him to just be quiet. I was trying to keep him calm and out of trouble. But he was not listening. The police told him to be quiet, but he just continued to talk. My daughter was screaming, "let him talk mom, don't say anything."

Because he kept running off at the mouth, his mouth got him in jail. To this day he will swear that it was our fault that he went to jail. Kevin's mouth sent him to jail.

He would not have gone to jail if he had listened to me, when I told him to be quiet and let the police deal with it. I didn't go to jail. The reason he went was because of his temper and his mouth.

He was always blaming me for everything that happened to him. "Our marriage is not going to work because of you," he would say. It was always me; always my fault for everything, let him tell it. He said, "I have nothing to do with our marriage not working out, it is all of your fault. It's only you." Now, how stupid is that? But he was the one with the other women. I never cheated or messed around. Not that I couldn't, but I fear God and I believe that a marriage is sacred and holy, not to be interrupted by outsiders. He was the one getting the pages and phone calls. But it's my "fault our marriage is not working?" Listen, when you open the door and let Satan into your holy matrimony, you are open game for anything to happen. Why do you think God tells us to rebuke Satan? That he will flee. We have to use the Word of God on the enemy to keep him out of our life, marriage, home and family.

Reflections

Communication is the key to every relationship. If you want yours to work, learn how to talk to each other; not <u>at</u> each other but <u>to</u> each other.

Get a clear understanding of what was spoken by the other person, and what was meant by what they spoke.

Sometimes we tend to hear things differently than the way they come out.

Because communication is a key factor in all relationships, you must have it in yours.

Kevin could never admit that there were issues he had going on in his life, so therefore, he will never be healed and delivered until he can admit there is a problem with him. If you don't think that there is anything wrong with you, why would you think there was a need for help, to be delivered and healed? Kevin's favorite words to me were, "Wives obey your husbands." My response was, "What about the rest of the verses in that same chapter, Ephesians 5:25 husbands love your wives, even as Christ also loved the church, and gave himself for it." He could not answer me.

We would fight and fuss like cats and dogs. He would go off on me and I in return went off on him putting one another down, trying to hurt the other ones' feelings. What good did it do? None! The devil won those times.

But there were times when God would win. We would be on our knees Praying, talking to God. Reading the bible together, studying for a class we were going to teach. We preached together and taught together. We ministered together as a team in the church and then get home and go at it. What kind of upside down, twisted around, stupid sided stuff is that? How can two people that say they know God, preach and teach God's Word, fight and not make up for weeks; not even talk to each other for weeks? I could never understand that, and I am sure I won't. That's some off stuff. I believe in what the Word of God says. Don't let the sun go down on your wrath. Which means I should be making up before the sun goes down? I would try that every time and when I tried that with him, he thought I was speaking a foreign language. He enjoyed the pleasure in holding his anger for days and weeks; sometimes months. That is what he preferred to do, and he did.

I remember about a few months after we got married his dad died. We had to go to Las Vegas to the funeral. We purchased two round trip air tickets to Las Vegas. After arriving in Las Vegas where his parents lived we were both to officiate at his father's funeral. Kevin did the eulogy and I assisted him. When it was time to leave, his mom told him he could have his dad's Dodge Caravan if he paid the notes that were due each month. He agreed to do so. So that meant we had to drive the van back to Detroit. Well, to be honest about it, I drove us back from Las Vegas. I think he may have driven about three hours, if that, during the total duration of our return. I drove over 72 hours.

It took us three days to make it back to Detroit. I saw day and night come and go for three days straight. We only pulled over to eat or for gas. We saw snow, sleet, hall, fog, rain, sun and clouds on our trip back. He woke me up when he was driving because he was scared of those high mountains and hills. I had been driving for hours and was sleepy and tired. I wasn't asleep thirty minutes when he called me. "Ruth, look!" I sat up and looked out the window. It was pitch black and my ears had started to pop because of the height of the mountains. I looked out and saw nothing but mountains. We were up so high on the mountains, going around and around. One wrong turn and we were over the edge. The worst thing about it was that it was pitch black outside and we couldn't see anything. So I talked to him until we got off those high mountains.

I started calling on the Lord to see us through. I would drive for hours and hours and when his turn came to drive he would drive for one hour and that was it, if that. That was the worst trip in my life. When we finally arrived home, I went straight to bed; it was hard trying to sleep in a van and get comfortable. I woke up in the middle of the night in shock! I screamed out, "Whose turn is it to drive?" He played me. He used me to do all the driving. Why? Because I told him I like to drive. I did before that.

Chapter 18

Abused by the Preacher

In this marriage like the previous one, I have been called every name but a child of God. Remember this is a man professing to be a man of God, a preacher and a pastor. I have been cursed out, spit on in the face, kicked, choked; hit in the face with his fist.

Kevin was 6' 2"; he weighted 290 pounds. I was a small, petite woman, 5' 3", and 115 pounds.

Reflections

God made man the stronger vessel. God designed the man's body different for many reasons. One was that they would carry the load, and be head of the house and deal with all things a man should, when his house is in divine order. Not to beat up on and put down the weaker vessel.

God made women the weaker vessel. He designed our bodies differently for a purpose. One purpose was to carry a child for nine months.

A man's structure is designed to carry the women in the time of trouble. Her body is not designed to carry him.

There are some full figured women, but they are still designed differently.

There are some small built men, but they are still designed to do what a man is supposed to do.

When the bills would come in I hated mentioning them to him because he would start an argument and leave. If I said, "The gas bill came, we owe $90.00." He would start fussing, asking me why did I tell him. He would say I was nagging. Hello, "I told you so it could get paid." A lot of men don't want to admit the truth. The truth is a man is to take care of his family. It is his responsibility.

If she works that's great. If she helps that's even better. But the bottom line is what the Word of God says. The man is the head. He is the provider.

His alliance is to his family. Make sure they have a roof over their head and clothes on their backs and food to eat. If the woman helps that's great.

Any woman that loves her husband is going to help to make ends meet. But that doesn't change the fact that the man is to take care of his wife. God said leave your mother and father and cleave to your spouse. You are no longer dad and mom's responsibility. Kevin became more and more disrespectful toward me.

We were on another trip to Las Vegas to visit his mom. We had a good time. It came time for us to leave; we were packed and ready to go. I looked at the tickets and they read, Friday. Today was Saturday. I could not believe I didn't check the return dates before then. I said, "We should have left yesterday." Do you know what this preacher who claims be a man of the cloth did? He called me every bad name that he could think of. He put me down in every way he could image in his mother's house. Instead of Kevin saying it's going to be okay, we will straighten it out, I was a dumb, stupid bitch, not thinking . . . . This man that professed to be a born again, child of God and who preached and taught God's Word, did this right in front of his mom. I was stunned, I though to myself, "What kind of person is this?" I guess it made him feel big when he reacted like that. He would do the same thing in front of his girls.

Some men feel big and bad when they put women down and when they abuse them. But really they are cowards and not real men. Men don't have to put a woman down to feel big. Men don't have to put their hands on a woman to feel big and bad.

Kevin had a vagabond spirit. That is when you can't stay in one place too long; you're always on the run. He would keep his clothes in big green garbage bags, because it would be easier for him to just grab his bags and leave. How sick is that? What's even sicker is that I put up with it, dealing with his sick issues, why? I continued trying to make our marriage work and I was not having any success. But it was doomed before we got married. His mind set was divorce.

I know that God hates divorces. But God does give releases for divorces. The Word gives us those reasons. Fornication is not the only reason one can get a bill of divorce.

We both were dealing with issues that desperately needed to be dealt with. So I suggested counseling.

We went, but he stopped because he said it wasn't anything wrong with him, it was all me and I needed to continue to go and seek help.

He would blame the accident that I was in; he said the hitting my head made me crazy. He would call me cripple. He started saying things like, "I see why William kicked your butt."

Reflections

If you're calling your spouse fat, skinny, ugly, baldhead, or any evil speaking towards them, you need to stop it! You need to repent and change those evil mean hateful words to kind and sweet soft words.

Proverbs 15:1 Talks about a soft answer turneth away wrath, but grievous words stir up anger. Phil 4:8 Whatsoever things are true, whatsoever things are honest, whatsoever things are just, whatsoever things are pure, whatsoever things are lovely, whatsoever things are of good report, if there be any virtue and if there be any praise, think on these things.

The devil wants you to talk about each other, down one another. Why? Becauseheisathief,hismissionistosteal,andtokill,andtodestroy.John10:10

He wants to destroy everything God has designed. God ordained marriage. So he wants to mock God, by causing Christians to belittle each other, disrespecting each other, and abuse each other.

The devil is a liar! He is the father of lies. You have to rebuke him and he will flee.

John 8:44

If you don't have anything good to say, then just don't say anything at all. Words can hurt, kill, steal and destroy.

Kevin always had something bad to say about all of my friends, every one of them. All of my friends had problems let him tell it.

Controlling people like to keep you isolated from everyone.

He had a construction business. He would remodel homes and do roofs on churches and on business.

I worked at an Advertising Agency for 15 years. They started laying people off. One year they added to my job when I was already doing 5 other people's jobs and did not want to give me a raise. I gave them my resignation three day's notice. Human Resources asked me to stay. I said, "I will if they give me a raise." They said they couldn't do more than the 3% that they had already offered me. I said, "Sorry, I can't stay more than three days."

I started my own cleaning business, Queen Esther Cleaning Services. I went out and got my accounts and employees. I had over 40 accounts and over 10 employees. Business was doing great. Kevin would tell me constantly, that I better not get sick and go into the hospital, because he wasn't going to run my business, because it wasn't his. He would say, "This is your business and you'd better take good care of yourself so you won't get sick." I wondered why he was always saying that, as if he was planning for me to get sick and go to the hospital. God kept me well.

Then I had to keep redoing jobs because the employees I had was not doing the job right. I had to fire everyone because I couldn't keep good help. I couldn't do all the work myself. I would ask him if he would help me so I would know how much to schedule for cleaning. He would tell me he would help clean so I would schedule a lot more than what I could do alone. And when the time came to clean he would start a fight so he could leave me cleaning alone. If I told him he didn't clean the stove or tub well enough he would leave. He would say, "I know how to clean." I would have four to six more apartments to clean by myself. I would be so tired. I would push myself and clean all of them. God gave me the strength to do it.

One time I had scheduled a lot of apartments to clean because I got his word that he was going to help me.

We got into an argument on the way to the apartments and I was left cleaning them all alone. He dropped me off. I had a vacuum, mops, brooms, buckets, towels and cleaning supplies that I had to drag from one side of the apartments to the other side because he left me without a car and help.

My daughter Kima, her husband and their five children lived across the street from the apartments that I was cleaning.

I took a break and walked over to their apartment. I was so tired and drained. My body was so weak I was shaking. I was hoping to get some help from her, but she couldn't leave; she didn't have a baby sitter. I called my other daughter, Tisha and asked if she could help, she couldn't help either. So there I was, stuck with six more apartments to clean alone.

It took hours just to clean one apartment. I did detail cleaning. I had to clean the stove, refrigerator, wash the cabinets out, sweep and mop the kitchen floor; sometimes the stove alone took hours to clean. I had to clean everything in the bathroom tub & shower, sink, everything. Sometimes the tub & shower took 2 or 3 hours to clean alone. I had to clean the blinds in the bedrooms (1-4), living room, and dinning room and then vacuum all these rooms, I had to wash all the windows in every room, patio doors inside and out and clean the tracks in the windows and doors. So when I say I had to clean, I really had to clean, detail cleaning was no joke. It would take 3 to 4 hours to clean what I would call a clean apartment. It could take 8 hours or more to clean a bad apartment.

So Kevin would tell me he was going to help me and do one, if that, and get mad about nothing and leave. Kevin pulled that trick twice, after that I didn't schedule more than what I could do alone. I would go and check the apartments and then give them my schedule. I learned from my mistakes. I used to just tell the apartment manager that I could clean 5 apartments without checking them out. When I get the keys to all five of the apartments and go check them out, some were clean, some okay and others were terrible. I think Kevin was trying to put me in the hospital. That didn't work, God kept me.

Kima wanted to help me when I came over to her apartment but she couldn't because she didn't have a baby sitter. I know she would have helped if she could've, even though she didn't like cleaning those apartments, it would make her sick to the stomach to see the filth in those terrible apartments. She told me later that after she saw me, how weak I looked, she cried when I left, because I looked like I was about to die. She just didn't know that I felt like I was about to die too. But God kept me! God blessed me with the strength to complete the job.

Kevin's excuse for leaving was, "Since I can't clean, I am gone." He would leave me with tons and tons of work to do. A lot of times I would just sit on the floor and cry and say God give me strength. And God would. And then I was able to finish the apartments. If that is not abuse, what is? What man would leave a woman to transfer all those cleaning products on foot? Not just any woman, but his wife? I am not an angel. I did some things that I am not proud of myself. Things like getting smart with him, going tit for tat; those types of things. I said things like, "Ugly, big nose, and big head." That was the extent of it. I didn't use dirty or vile words. I never cursed.

I remember one day his daughter's mom called me and told me that she and Kevin was back together. After I hung up the phone I threw every piece of wedding items we had in the trash. I trashed everything, picture albums, video, wedding glasses, knife, everything. When I talked to him I told him what she had said to me, of course he denied it. I thank God I was determined that I was not going to go back into that same state where my first husband had me, which was low self esteem. I know who I am, and whom I belong to. God is love and He is my all! The Great I AM! He is my provider, my comforter and my protector. He keeps making ways out of no way. When those horrible name-callings and beatings took place, I still refused to go back to having low self-esteem. I remind myself that I am somebody! I am a child of the most-high God! I know that if nobody loves me, God does! I constantly reminded myself that I am fearfully and wonderfully made.

Kevin could be sweet at times and bitter at other times.

I really liked the Honda Accord, I kept saying, "I am going to have a Honda Accord; I could see it in my driveway. I would say, "I see my blue Honda Accord in the driveway."

One day Kevin came home and said, "Go get you a car, I will give you the down payment and you will have to make the payments." I didn't act on it, and he would keep telling me, "I told you to go get your car."

So finally, I went to Page Toyota and picked out a light blue Honda Accord. He gave me the down payment and I paid the car notes.

Kevin and I separated so often, every time I left or he left me God would always bless me with a place to stay. I would get back with my husband and let him move in with me and I would always lose my place, as if he was a curse to me.

When we moved from Oak Park with my daughters, we moved to the Coach House Apartments in Southfield, and got evicted from there. He knew that we were getting put out and he left the day they were scheduled to put our belongings out on the street. My furniture and all my belongings got put out on the curb and he wasn't there with me. He came to the apartment later to help me get the things to storage. Kevin would always leave when the heat was turned up or in pressured situations.

We moved so many times; I can't tell you how many addresses I've had. You just don't know how many phone numbers I have had. From lease property to hotels, which was the place he most felt comfortable in. We would pay from $350-$450 plus a week to stay in these hotels. I eventually paid off what we owed to the Coach House Apartments. He didn't give me one penny towards paying that debt off. Then I lived in the Laurel Woods Apartments, we were not together when I signed the lease. I asked him if he would help me move in, he did. A few weeks later he was moving in with me. My daughter, her husband and their five children moved in with me. They didn't have to pay rent, but just help with the gas and light bills. Because she had five babies, it would get loud in the apartment; I warned them that I would get put out if they couldn't keep the children quiet. It is not easy keeping small children quiet, but it can be done. When I let my husband move in he said, "They need to find someplace to live, because we will all get put out." The noise continued, I told my daughter they had to move. It was always hard doing something like that. They would help me out by letting me move in with them and not having to pay rent; I would help them by letting them move in with me. That's what families are for. If you can't depend on your family members, then who can you depend on?

They found a house and moved in it. It's great to have open space when you have little children. If you have children they need space to run and play if possible, but sometimes it's not possible and you have to work with what you have. It wasn't long before I got put out of that apartment. This time I moved my things out before they set them out. Kevin told me he had the money, but because he was mad at me he wasn't going to give it to me. I did not fall for that lie. I said, "So you're telling me that you can prevent us from getting put out and because you are angry, you won't!" He's the provider or should be. He didn't have it. If he did, his intentions were to bring me down.

One night before we got evicted Kima came over, he got mad about something and told her to get out, she said something back and he picked her up and pushed her out of the house.

Reflections

Men, please do your job as a husband. You are the provider. Nothing should cause you to allow your family to go without. Don't let anger or anything dictate your support to your family.

Woman, please, we must stay in our place, by allowing the man to be the man. What we should be doing is praying for that man. If your man is not stepping up to the plate and being the head, then you have to do what you have to do for yourself and your family.

We don't have to put up with abuse. If that man is telling you to do something that doesn't line up with the Word of God, you don't have to do it. We cripple the men by doing their job. Let him do it. He is the head. When men do their part, it makes it easier for the women to do her part. That works both ways.

After I got evicted from Laurel Woods Apartments, I moved in with my baby brother, Kevin and his second wife, Jane, and their two children.

I stayed there for awhile and after awhile my husband and I started talking again. I paid my brother $500 a month; I slept in the basement. They had a very beautiful home in Farmington Hills. My husband, Kevin, moved in my brother's house with me and we paid $550 a month. The rent went up $50 with him moving in.

My husband's mother came to town for a week. He asked her to co-sign for him so he could move in The Lakes Apartments. My credit wasn't good enough; neither was his. So his mom co-signed for him. They wouldn't do it in his name, only in my name. He wanted his name on the lease, but they wouldn't allow it.

Not only did she co-sign for us to get the apartment, she charged over $3,000 worth of furniture for our new apartment. I thought things were starting to look up.

A few months after we moved in together, Kevin jumped on me and then put me out. He said, "Get out of my house!"

Let me tell you what happened. It was Wednesday night after Bible study. The service was awesome; God was in that place. The anointing was so strong in the sanctuary that everyone in there was laid out prostrate before God.

I was the Sunday School Superintendent. I had a planned meeting with the teachers. I was in the back pews talking to one of the teachers; the meeting had not started yet. Kevin was standing at the end of the pew. He wanted to get by and I was talking, so I didn't move and asked if he could go around. I could have moved, but I didn't. That was selfish on my part; I was wrong. The devil was busy after that anointed service. He was working on the both of us. I finally moved, had my meeting and left the church. As I was walking to the parking lot, still at the church, he started cursing me out and calling me all kind of names. I had embarrassed him in front of the women I was talking to.

We got to The Lakes Apartments and I knew, how he was acting, I was not going in the apartment with him. So I said, "I'm going to get me something to eat." That didn't work; he snatched my car keys out of my hands. He came around to the driver's side where I was seated. He pulled me out of the car. He pulled me by my hair from the car to the apartment, which was about a block away from where I had parked my car. He was pulling and dragging me by my hair until we got to the door of our apartment. When we got to the door, he let me go and went upstairs. He didn't want anyone to see him pulling me up the stairs. He didn't know what I was going to do going up the stairs, so he let me go. I stood downstairs in the entrance hall; he had my keys so I couldn't leave. I didn't know what to do or where to go. I stood there, "Where do I go?" I didn't want to go up to the apartment with him, and I didn't know anyone nearby. So I stood there for a while, thinking.

With nowhere to go, I went upstairs. As soon as I stepped in the door he pulled me in and started hitting me with his fist, slapping me, and choking me. He took his fist and beat me in my head, in my face. Then he just stopped and told me to get out, I tried to tell him I loved him, thinking he would stop, but he got worse. I didn't understand why he was doing this. He said, "You always act like you don't do anything." I didn't move out of his way, is that what made that hateful demon loose? He told me to call my girlfriend Sherri. He said we were lesbians. He said, "Tell her to come get you out of my house." I told him he should go to sleep and think about what he was asking me to do. He said, "I know what I am doing, get out."

He started again, beating on me so I called Sherri. It was late, we got out of church at 9:00, then I had the teachers meeting. Sherri was at church also, she was one of the teachers so she was at the meeting too. It had to be about 10:00 pm or 11:00 pm. I called crying, "Sherri, can you come get me?"

She said, "What's wrong?"

I said, "He's beating me up!"

She said, "I will be there."

She was in bed; she got up, got dressed and came to pick me up. She came in trying to talk to him, "What's going on? Calm down!" She was talking to him.

He started with her; "You shut up and get her out of here!"

"What's the problem?" she said.

She tried again talking to him, trying to calm him down, I said, "Sherri, please, don't say anything, let's just go, and let me get a few outfits." I grabbed a few of my things and we left. I explained everything to her on the way to her place and continued after we arrived at her apartment.

That same night, after jumping on me and putting me out, Kevin had the nerve to come over to Sherri's apartment. He rang the doorbell. We didn't let him in. He called my cell phone and said, "I am sorry, I made a mistake, come home." Is that sick or what?

That's right, he was sorry and he had made a mistake. I was not going back to that house with him ever, so I thought. Sherri and I worked together and went to the same church. I didn't have my car because she came and picked me up plus he had my car keys. This was my car, the one I paid for. I had a lot of cars, from brand new to very old.

He beat my butt, put me out and took my car, this man that professed to be a pastor and preacher. I know he's human, but where was the fear of God? I called him and told him that if he didn't drop my car off that I was going to report it as stolen. He dropped my car off.

We both were Elders at the church where we attended. I called our Bishop and told her he had jumped on me and put me out. She said, "We will have to talk."

Bishop didn't say anything else to me; she wouldn't talk to me. I didn't understand why.

I kept trying to sat up an appointment with her so we could talk but I kept getting the brush-off.

Kevin left the church and didn't come back. I didn't leave.

The Elder that we were under could not understand why I wouldn't go back to Kevin.

After months of being separated I called Kevin and told him he needed to file for a divorce because I was going to start seeing other men. That Sunday after service he was waiting outside to talk to me. He started asking me whom was I seeing; I told him not anyone yet, but men are enquiring and I am going to start dating.

When I came to this church, I started a prison ministry with a team of Ministers, one man and a four women. We would go to visit the women in prison every other month. Kevin was not apart of the prison ministry because he was not cleared. Something on his record prevented him from being cleared to come with us. Bishop stopped me from going to the prison; she set me down and told me that I couldn't do anything in the ministry. I didn't understand why I was being sat down when I didn't do anything. He jumped on me. I was obedient to Bishop and set down in the church for months without doing anything. Why? Because my husband had jumped on me and put me out of our home. She still wouldn't sit down and talk to me for weeks, I really needed to talk to her, but she wouldn't talk to me. I kept calling trying to schedule an appointment, but I never was able to do so. I finally got an appointment with her. I told her just what happened and she said, "sometimes we cause it on ourselves." I didn't understand that, my understanding is that a man should never put his hands on a woman for any reason, and she should keep her hands off of him.

So I called the church back and cancelled my appointment. I told them I wasn't yet released from my church. I was teaching Bible class at my job once a week and my supervisor said you may have missed your calling because you can teach. She asked me if I knew that I was called to teach, I told her "yes". She then suggested that I apply for the assistant pastor at her church. I did; I got a resume' together and sent it in and the church called, they said they liked my resume' and was calling to set up an appointment. We set a date and time. I was trying to talk to the Bishop about it and still Couldn't get an appointment with her. I prayed about it and I was released to move on. I tried to get an appointment with her to tell her that it was time for me to move on. I couldn't get an appointment for weeks again.

When I sent word to her that I was leaving, she still didn't have the time to talk to me. I finally got an appointment with her. I was there and she was on the run still. I had to take a ride with her because she had another appointment. So there we sat, in her SUV, Bishop and a female Elder and me. Bishop and I sat in the back as the Elder drove. We talked; she said I should get my divorce. She said I didn't need to leave because I could have two churches. I asked her, if I did that, which church would I tithe to? She said, "Let God lead you."

Chapter 19

The Preacher is a Con-Artist

Kevin would come home stressed out and tired. With his job as a construction Worker, along with conning people, he was stressed out. Not only was Kevin the Preacher man, he was good at remodeling homes and churches. Not only was he preaching the Word of God, he also had another profession that I was not aware of until he stole from me. I told you about my cleaning company, "Queen Esther Cleaning Service." He would help me clean some of the offices. This is my husband, I trusted him. I never thought for one second he would steal from me.

He got busted one morning so he had to spill the beans about his other trade.

One evening he came in and said, "I got caught." I said, "Got caught, doing what?" He said, "I would go in stores and take their products and sell them." The store owner's thought that he was a retailer that would come in and take the old items and restock it with new items. He used to work at Brown and Williams doing this type of work, so that's where he got the idea I guess. He said he had been doing it for a while.

Then he told me he had been taking checks from one of my clients, the lawyer's office, and he had been writing himself checks and cashing them. He had been getting away with it until he got caught this one day. He said, "I went to the bank, they took my license and called the police. I ran out." The only reason he told me was because he got caught. I don't know what else he did or who he had stolen from. I could not believe that he would take from my clients. As soon as he told me I called my client, that he stole the checks from, and told him everything I knew. He was so nice about it. He allowed me to continue to work for him. He said, "It's not your fault, and you didn't do anything." He said, "We have insurance that will cover that."

Kevin had already been going back and forth to court with his lawyer for another case. He never wanted me to get involved with it nor did he want me to go to court with him. He wouldn't even tell me what it was about. I eventually found out that Kevin had been writing bad checks, taking money out their bank accounts. His customers and my clients were his victims. He would use his business the remodeling as a cover up. He would get the jobs working on their house and then he would get them to trust him. He would tell them he was a Pastor. He would always talk about Jesus Christ to them, so they trusted him.

They would trust him with their keys to their homes, churches and businesses. Allowing him to work on their property at his leisure; thinking everything was alright. When he should have been working, instead he was going through their personal items, and drawers looking for their checkbooks, credit cards anything he could take, and get cash for. It is scary, I never knew I was married to such a man.

He would have me write checks when we both knew the money wasn't in the bank. He would tell me he would give me the money back when he completed the job. He would always "have the money tomorrow," but tomorrow never came. Then I would get in trouble because I bounced the checks. He would always have a good excuse why he didn't have the money. He was good at lying and cheating people. He had no fear of God. I remember I would ask him, "Don't you fear God?" He could never answer me.

Jessie Haddon, my brother-in-law, worked for him. Jessie would help him out when he got in binds or just need an extra hand. Jessie was good in carpentry also. It came time for Jessie to get paid and Kevin gave Jessie a check. Jessie went to the bank to cash the check, and could have gotten in trouble just for trying to cash a check that was not his to cash. I never really knew the whole story, only bits and pieces of it from what I heard them talking about. And I only know about that because Jessie kept telling Kevin that he was mad at him for what he did, he gave him a check that belonged to someone else. I told Kevin, Jessie could have gotten in trouble just for trying to cash the check. Jessie was so mad at Kevin about that incident. Kevin kept telling Jessie he was going to take care of him. I don't think he ever did.

Kevin would have so much money at times and other times he would have nothing.

He was stressed because he was stealing from the people he worked for.

Reflections

Lesson: Just because men/women have titles as: Bishop, Rev., Elder, Pastor, Deacon, Minister, ... they are human first. Just because they're always talking about Jesus Christ, means that they really love Him or even know Him. Don't be so quick to put your trust in people just because they mention the name of God. You must get to know them. There are evil men and women out here hiding behind the name, Jesus Christ, using titles and pulpits to pimp the church and God's people.

Don't misunderstand me, there are still many true, honest and loving god fearing men and women around and you will know them by their fruits.

It's one thing to be called by God to preach his Word. It's another thing for you to call yourself to preach God's Word.

Many people today are doing just that. God did not call them; they called themselves.

They use God as a cover up. They hide behind the name of God.

The devil knows God and the Word of God. But does he follow God? "No!"

The devil will disguise himself as an angel in sheep's clothing.

Remember, the enemy cares about no one. He has one set goal! That is to get all he can for himself and destroy all others.

We work hard for our homes and to furnish them, and then someone comes in and steals our belonging.

We work hard to start our own businesses and ministries, and then others come in and destroy what God has blessed us with.

Please, be careful with those you fall so quickly in love with; those into whose hands you trust your children to, and those you let pray over and for you.

Pray and Seek God before you're so willing to give into them and their word alone. Because it sounds good, or it feels right, that doesn't mean that it is.

If someone treats you wrong, God will handle them. The battle belongs to God.

You may have been one of those people that stole from someone or maybe someone has stolen from you.

Regardless of who took from who, let it go.

You have to forgive them. First, forgive yourself and then forgive them.

Don't let anyone or anything keep you from entering into heaven.

If you pray, God will reveal to you those whom you need to forgive.

Kevin got over on a lot of people. For everyone that he has stolen from and taken from, he will pay. Kevin took over $3,000 from my client at the lawyer's office. That's only what I know about, I don't know for sure how much he took.

God, and the integrity that He has blessed me with, is the only reason I didn't lose that account. The owner gave me a great compliment. He said, "I know you and I enjoy working with you." "You have been with us and I can trust you."

I started losing my accounts. It started happening all about the same time. I would get a call, from one of my clients, telling me that my services were no longer needed, without any explanation. I figured it out after everything came out in the open that Kevin had been stealing from them so they let my company go. I remember saying to Kevin, "I don't know what is happening. All of a sudden, I'm losing all my accounts. He didn't say a word, but he knew why. I fear God too much to treat people dishonestly and to hurt God's people.

God said, "Vengeance is mine." If someone hurts you and misleads you or handles you in the wrong matter, God will handle it.

I remember when I first gave my life to God. I had to go to one of my girlfriend's house and ask her to forgive me. I had spread a rumor that was not true and after accepting Jesus Christ as my personal savior, I had to go and tell her what I had did and ask her to forgive me.

I did and she did forgive me.

I told you this because we all have some deep down hidden secret that we need to apologize for. We have to forgive and go on with our lives. unforgiviness keeps us bound to that person, until we forgive them. In releasing them, you release yourself. We will not be forgiven by God if we don't forgive. Loose yourself, and that person, right now and let them go, forgive them!

I was able to forgive with God's help!

Chapter 20

Money Can't Get You Into Heaven

Before we left our former church where we both were Elders. Kevin spent over $20,000.00 on the Bishop for her birthday celebration. What did we get in return? We got put out of our house and had to move into a hotel.

Kevin said to me out of the blue, "I want Bishop to have a great birthday celebration, and I am going to give her one."

I said okay. It sounded good to me, but I thought that he meant to get a committee together and all the Elders and leaders of the church she was the Bishop over would come together and put in a portion for Bishop's birthday celebration.

So I talked to a few Elders and leaders of the church. There were a few that said they would help us. But as the time got closer and I tried to set up a meeting for us to discuss what we would do, everyone that said they would help had backed out.

So that left Kevin and me.

I don't know why or what caused Kevin to go out of his way to spend over $20,000.00 on another woman for her birthday is beyond me! He never spent nowhere near that kind of money on me.

When I mentioned it to him, he brushed me off and said "I am doing it, if I have to do it by myself." Kevin was a show off. He liked to play big-timer. Make people think he had it going on like that, when he really didn't, if he did, I didn't know about it. So we started the planning things like, where it would be held, and who would we use for entertainment. If that wasn't enough, he also gave her the money to buy her a designer outfit. He gave me $1,000 to take her for her dress. When I got over to her house I was not invited inside, I was met at the door and her assistant took the money from me. It was in the winter and it was freezing outside. She could have invited me inside out of the cold. I was not asked to come in, even though I was an Elder at the church. My dress for her birthday celebration cost him only $69.00.

During the same time Kevin was so free and willing to give Bishop a birthday celebration, we had three months to be out of the house where we were living.

I found a house in the newspaper. It stated that the house would be rented for six months to one year. I went to look at the house and I fell in love with it. It was in Farmington Hills, Michigan. It was a four bedroom three bathroom home. It had one acre of land in the backyard and about a half acre in the front. It had a fireplace, and all appliances were included. Everything I always wanted. Even though I knew it was for only six months to one year.

We both had our own businesses and $1,050.00 was nothing for us to pay monthly. We needed $3,000 to move in and rent payment would be $1,050.00.

We definitely didn't have it to be doing, but he said, "I felt led." We had income coming in, but we had to pay our employees and bills. Neither one of us was good with saving or managing our money. So I borrowed the $3,000 from my baby brother Kevin and I paid him back. My husband, Kevin, did not give me one penny in the payback. But yet he could spend $20,000.00 on another woman for her birthday. There is something for sure wrong with this picture. We were renting from these very nice people who owned Fuddruckers. We had six months to one year to stay there because the house was going to be torn down and a Shopping Mall was going to be built there. All the homeowners in that area were offered a lump sum of money for their property.

How could Kevin commit to such a large celebration, when he knew that within a few months we had to be moved out of that house? What Kevin should've been doing with that kind of money; was looking for a place for his family to live.

I don't really know Kevin's real motive for the expensive celebration party, whether he wanted to be seen or if he was having an affair. I honestly don't think he was, but I do know you just don't give that kind of money away, unless God speaks to you. And believe me, when God is in it, you will be blessed, not cursed! That is why it is so important to sow into good ground. Because you reap what you sow. For he that soweth to his flesh shall of the flesh reap corruption; but he that soweth to the Spirit shall of the Spirit reap life everlasting. Galatians 6:8

People don't just spend $20,000.00 on a birthday celebration when they really don't have it. But he sure did come up with that money. Sure, people spend that and more, but only if they got it like that! I missed every penny of that money spent for a birthday celebration. Why? Because we didn't have it, because we needed it to move. He paid for the hall that was in Bloomfield Hills, Michigan. He paid for all the tickets and the money from the purchase of each ticket was to go to her for her birthday.

And do you know Bishop's assistant, the same one that would not let me in the Bishops house, had the nerve to ask me if we were going to pay for a ticket. If that isn't creed, what is? I didn't even answer that ridiculous question. How could she even form her mouth to ask such a foolish, outrageous question? After all the money we had spent, she sounded really crazy. He paid for the limo, for her to be picked up and dropped off. Then that same assistant blamed the limo driver for stealing her money. Which he didn't; she found it later that evening.

We got a letter in the mail telling us that we had 30 days to be moved out; that the demolition of the house was going to start in 30 days and we had to be out. We went looking for houses. We found one that we really loved and I was approved. All we needed was $2,500.00 to move in and neither one of us had it. He could've at least put something aside for our down payment on a house. He was too busy trying to impress people. I just knew he had it somewhere; he just needed to go get it. He told me he didn't have it. I wanted to faint. I didn't believe him. I couldn't accept that. Not after he just dished out thousands and thousands of dollars for one celebration.

I just know that if he could give someone else that kind of money, surely he had money for a place to lay his own head, right? "Wrong, he didn't have it!" When I give, I give from my heart. I give not expecting anything in return. But I do think this was a bit much, because Kevin or I didn't have it to give.

I was so out done. Here it is, time for us to move and we don't have money to use for a down payment. What kind of stuff is that? I told him, "You'd better call Bishop and see if she can help you." He called her and I listened on the other line. Her words, "It ain't going down like that, you will not be set out on the streets." She had the money but wasn't willing to help us out. Not only did we give her a $20,000.00 birthday celebration, I gave $2,000 for the building fund when I first came to the church. So that the church could be paid off. Not only that, Kevin and I would give our tithes plus $100 each week just in offering. Like I said earlier, It is very important where you sow your seed. If you're not sowing on good ground, your seed will not prosper. You will not have a harvest. Hear me. And you mean to tell me you can't give up $2,500.00 for us to move in or something towards that, for us to move into a house. Her only words to us were, "it won't go down like that." No prayer for us; no let me see what I can do to help you, nothing.

That's the reason people are leaving these churches today because it seems like the people are being ripped off in some churches. Not all churches are like this. The Bishop didn't even say, "Let me pray for you." It was not the streets, but we were homeless. We had to move into the Candlewood Suites, where we paid $450 a week for one room. We paid more every month at the hotel than what we paid for the four-bedroom home we had in Farmington Hills.

Reflections

Beloved, don't think that you can buy love, friendship or relationships. whether it is in church, on your job or with someone you meet.

You can't buy love. You can't buy your way into Heaven.

Don't even try it. Don't try to get ahead by giving more money.

If you do, what are you going to do when the money runs out?

I went through a horrible ordeal, where my husband took from our household to be seen or to look good. For whatever reason he did it, I know for a fact that we really didn't have it.

Were did it get us? It got us nowhere, and without a roof over our heads.

When you truly love someone just be yourself.

Being you is so much easier.

God is not a respecter person, neither should we be.

Chapter 21

The Preacher Strikes Out

My husband Kevin and I got back together for a few months and after that he put me out of the Lakes Apartments where we were living. I moved in with Sherri.

He was staying at the Day's Inn Hotel in Southfield. I moved in there with him. We were paying $350 a week to stay in a hotel with one room.

Things were going okay. One night while I was on the phone with my daughters on the three-way, they heard us arguing, so they called Alfonzo. Alfonzo and Larry, my son and son-in-law, came over to the hotel.

They gave us a pep talk. In short, they said we were too old for this foolishness. Larry said, "A woman needs security." He was right; I didn't want to keep moving from hotel to hotel. I wanted a home, somewhere we could settle down.

They asked me if I wanted to leave, I said, "No, we weren't fighting, we just had a disagreement." They made sure I was okay and they left. Then a few weeks later, it was my side of the family's family reunion, which was held at Belle Isle. I asked Kevin if he was going with me. His response was, "No, I don't know those people." Mind you, we had been married for 14 years and we have the same family reunion each year, only in different locations.

The reunion was always on a Sunday. I woke up praising God and giving Him thanks.

I asked Kevin if he was going to go to church with me. He said, "No." I got dressed and went to my girlfriend Ivy's church service; she had invited me; I went to the 8:00 a.m. service and I also went to my normal 11:00 morning service at my church. I picked up my grandchildren after the 11:00 service so they could go to the picnic with me.

My grandchildren and I went back to the hotel so I could change clothes. When I got there Kevin started arguing about my being gone so long and taking the car. He asked, "What am I supposed to do while you're at the picnic?"

I didn't say a word; I had to use the restroom so I went to the bathroom and closed the door. He burst in through the bathroom door and grabbed me by my neck and started cursing me out. My grandchildren were in the next room. They could hear everything. I was so upset. I still didn't say a word. I came out of the bathroom, got my clothes and got dressed. I was trying to hold back the tears, but couldn't. We left for the picnic in my car.

I was so hurt. How could he, in front of my grandchildren? The more I thought about it the more the tears came rolling down my cheeks. My grandchildren tried to encourage me and lift me up. One said, "Grandma, are you alright?"

Full and trying to hold back the tears I didn't want to speak because I would have burst out crying. I nodded, "Yes."

While still driving, heading to the picnic, my cell phone rang, It was Kevin calling, he said, "I'm sorry come back and pick me up." He wanted to go now that he thought about what he had done. I told him it was over and I was not coming back. I got to Belle Isle and had red marks on my neck from where he choked me; my eyes were red from crying. My cousin came over and said, "Ruth, you can do better; you don't have to put up with that." I didn't say a word to anyone about what had happened; I had just got there. I didn't have to say a word; it was obvious that I had been in a fight.

After I left the picnic I went to the police station, the police escorted me to the hotel to get my clothes. I moved in with my daughter Kima, her husband Larry and their five children. I was only there for one week and God blessed me with an apartment in Warren. I moved in and my baby daughter, Tisha, moved in with me. I was there for awhile when Kevin and I started talking again.

Reflections

It was an addiction to the abuse. No, I didn't like it nor did I want it, but I kept going after it. Do drug addicts like what they do? No, but they are addicted.

Regardless of how bad I was treated or how low I was brought down. I didn't understand at the time while I was in the abuse. It was not until I was out of it, was I able to see the truth. Being addicted to something is not necessarily something you enjoy doing, nor want to do, nor go through.

When you do something long enough it becomes additive, and habit forming. good or bad. I thought I was in love, I felt like it would stop and we would go on with our lives. That's just it; it doesn't just stop, it gets worse and worse. They tell you they are sorry and that it won't happen again, but it's just a lie. The abuser is just as addicted as the one being abused. They don't want to, but it's a habit; an addiction. The abuser and the victim both need serious help and healing.

God would be a great place to start if you or someone you know needs help.

Kevin and I talked about getting back together. He told me I could move in with him in Detroit, in an upstairs flat where he was living. He was telling me about some of the things going on there, like how he didn't control the heating and other things that were not acceptable living to me. I told him that I had a nice apartment in Warren and I just moved in not too long ago and I couldn't move out and break my lease.

God was trying to show me again that I needed to move on with my life.

We had not seen or talked to each other for months. He called me and we started talking about where we lived. We made plans to go out to dinner. I drove around and around and could not find his flat. I called him and told him I was headed back home because I can not find his flat, I said, "I think we need to forget about dinner, and go our separate ways." I said, "It must be a reason I can't find you." So he asked me to keep trying that he really wanted it to work this time and he explain how to get to his flat again and I went back and found it but I should have stuck with my decision after I couldn't find it.

Kevin had been messing around with the lady that lived downstairs from him. I found that out after he had moved in with me. She called me and told me about it. Of course Kevin denied it.

My brother-in-law, Jessie, said he had something he wanted to tell me. I told Kevin, and he said he wanted to tell me about some girl. He said if Jessie told on him that he was going to tell Rose, my sister, on Jessie. He didn't realize that just by saying that alone, he was telling on himself. Satan will have you dipping and dapping in sin and make you look like a fool without recognizing how foolish you look.

We got back together the end of 2003 and in January 2004 he moved in with my daughter and me. The lady that lived downstairs from him called my cell phone again and tried to tell me that Kevin was a big liar. She said, "He drove my car and broke it. She said, "he told me he was going to fix it and never did." She told me all the things he said about me, how he put me down and said he was getting a divorce.

My daughter had got married. Her and her husband lived with us for a few months, before getting their own new apartment.

Kevin and I were at our new church home working in the ministry. It was in July, when our Pastor asked Kevin if he would bring the Word on Sunday Morning. He said, "Yes." Kevin and I did a tag team preaching many times. Sometimes he would preach and I would come behind him and pray for God's people. That is what we did at our church, on Sunday, July 4, 2004.

On Monday, July 5, 2004, the fourth of July Holiday weekend. Kevin invited his daughters over for dinner at our place. He went to pick them up. They ate and watched some television. It started getting late and they were ready to leave.

Kevin asked me if I wanted to ride with him to take them home, I told him no, I wanted to clean up, wash dishes and get ready for work the next day.

Kevin and the girls were in the kitchen fixing their plates to go. His grandson, the oldest daughter's son, was playing and jumping on the pillow that was in the living room on, the floor. He slipped and fell down and started crying. Kevin looked out from the kitchen and asked me what did I do? I looked at him as if he were crazy. "I didn't do anything." Why is it that I had to have done anything? Children play, and hurt themselves, cry, and get up playing again before you know it.

But instead of him coming in and asking me what had happened he asked me what I did. I shouted back to him, "I didn't do anything!" He came out of the kitchen and started calling me names and getting in my face. I got up and went into the bedroom. He came in the bedroom calling me out my name, "You stupid bitch, what's wrong with you, you don't know how to watch a baby." I started putting up the clothes that I had washed earlier that day. The drawers were old so in order to close them I had to slam it.

He started screaming; he said, "If you slam another drawer I will beat your butt."

First of all, this fool done forgot where he was. He was in my house trying to play mister big stuff in front of his daughters.

He grabbed me by my neck and pushed me up against the wall, calling me bitch and other unheard of names. I was so shocked and undone. I couldn't believe he would act like that again, and in front of his girls, and in my house, and we had just gotten back together in December 2003. It had only been seven months. Well, seven is complete/perfection.

As the girls were leaving out they said, "Bye Ruth." I said, "Bye." I guess they didn't hear me, or Kevin didn't hear me, so he came in the room and said, "Did you hear my daughters talking to you?" I knew then after that, he was definitely trying to show off in front of his girls. As soon as they left the house I called my daughter, Tisha, I told her what had just happened and I called the police. I needed a ride because he took the car that we were both renting to get back and forth to work for $400 a week. That is some sick stuff, leasing a car for that kind of money. I kept telling him, with that type of money, we could have gotten our own cars fixed.

That was it, preacher man had struck out. He had put his hand on me for the last time. I'd had enough, and I was fed up. That wasn't the first incident.

There was no hope. The more I tried to fight for the marriage, the more he was fighting against it. His affairs and abuse had ended that day with me.

I called the police after hanging-up with Tisha. I told them what had happened; I told them I would call them when he got back.

When Tisha got to my apartment I went outside and sat in the car until Kevin returned. I saw him pulling into the driveway; I called the police and told them that he was in the apartment.

The police pulled up and I got out of the car and took them upstairs to my apartment. They knocked on the door, he asked, "Who is it?"

"Police," they replied.

He opened the door and we all went in, the two officers and I.

They asked, "What seems to be the problem?"

"My wife and I had a little disagreement." Kevin said.

I said, "No, he choked me."

They told me to keep quiet. They told Kevin to empty his pockets, and he did. They searched him to see if he had a weapon on him. Then they continued to ask him questions,

I kept saying, "He's lying." So they told me to leave out. So I went to my daughter's car.

They came out with him in handcuffs and put him in the police car. He was arrested because he had warrants out for his arrest. I had to fill out a police report about the incident.

He did one month for the abuse done to me. He did one year for the other crimes that he had committed. He called the church we attended and asked the pastor if I was taking my medication. He was trying to make it seem as if I had a problem and was on some type of medication. He was the one taking the medication; he had just been diagnosed with diabetes. Kevin had an addiction to medication. He would drink cough medicine and take pain pills regularly. That was his problem; he was on drugs.

That was truly the last straw for me. I filed for my divorce and had every right. Not only was he an abuser, he was an adulterer. I spent 29 ½ years married to two abusive men. Today I am free, thank God; I am free from being abused, put down, belittled and physically beat up.

I am no longer addicted to abuse. God healed and delivered me!
God is a deliverer!

Reflections

I am not perfect. I am far from it. God is still working with me!

What I've learned from all of this is that just because someone is treating you badly and unfairly, you don't have to react the same way. God said "And we know that all things work together for good to them that love God, to them who are the called according to his purpose." Romans 8:28

God will fight your battle. Let Him! You exemplify Jesus Christ if you are a born again believer. 2 Corinthians 5:17—"Therefore if any man be in Christ, he is a new creature: old things are passed away; behold, all things are become new."

The way you used to handle situations, the language you used to use, cheating and stealing from others, you should not be doing any of that. Why, because you are now a new person. You have Christ Jesus and your desire is to please God. God will move on your behalf every time if you will allow Him to.

We all have to answer to God for every idle word that we speak out of our mouth. That is why it is so important to watch what we say.

I was treated unfairly and wrong in both my relationships. I have decided to let God fight my battle. You see the battle is not yours, it is the Lord's.

We must do our part: forgive, and move on. Then God will forgive us. When we don't forgive, we are then bound to that person. Release them as well as yourself and be free.

God released me from both my previous marriages.

For all you who think that adultery is the only reason in the Bible for one to divorce, keep reading your Bible and you will find there is more than that reason where God will release you from a marriage.

I don't think anyone should get divorced just because they're tired of one another or they feel they have out-grown each other, or any reason that is outside of what the Bible speaks of.

God knew what married people would do; how they would get married for all the wrong reasons and then want out. He saw the cheating. Being God He knows all things and He is everywhere at the same time, He gave the reasons a man or woman could file for a divorce.

Men let God send your mate. Women let God direct you in making that choice. Sometimes the counterfeits come before the real treasure.

Marriage is wonderful when it is shared with the right one, with God, with love, when you care and have respect for each other. I cannot say it enough, "Wait on God!" "Include God!" There is a generational curse that needs to be broken from my family blood line. Divorce is running rampant in my family line and I take authority over it NOW! In the Name of JESUS! I command it to cease. I bind up that spirit of divorce and loose a spirit of commitment in our marriages. I will be married to my dear sweet wonderful husband, Pastor Clarence T. Webb, until God takes us home. You can do the same for any generational curse that is in your family. Just take authority over in the Name of Jesus. God said, whatsoever we bind on earth He has bound it in heaven and whatsoever we loose on earth he has loosed it in heaven. Matthew 16:19

God has given us the authority and He will not do for us what he has already given us to do!

God Bless You! Be free from any and all addictions! In Jesus Name!

Kima and the Amikad Fashion Show

"Accomplishments"
Amikad Designs Fashion Show
Kima is the Owner & Designer of Amikad Designs,
these are a few pictures for one of her fashion shows.

Kima and myself

Kima

Kima

Kima on the microphone, thanking the people for coming to the show
Behind Kima, with the white t-shirt on is my niece, Amanda;
next to Amanda is Rose, my sister; next to Rose is myself

Kima holding the Roses and my sister, Rose

My sister Rose

Top: My brother Roy and his wife and my mother
Second: Kima and Tisha
Bottom: Me in the center; smallest girl is Kima; tallest is Tisha

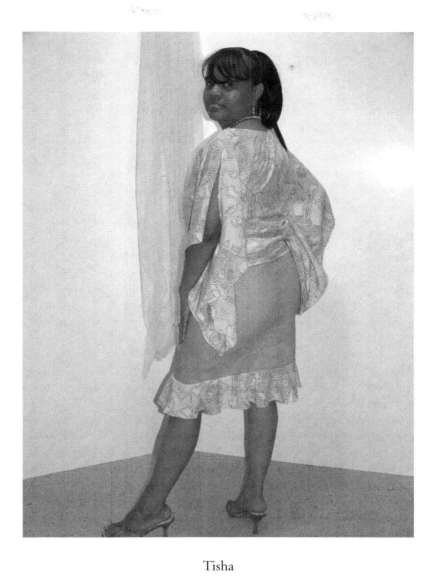

Tisha

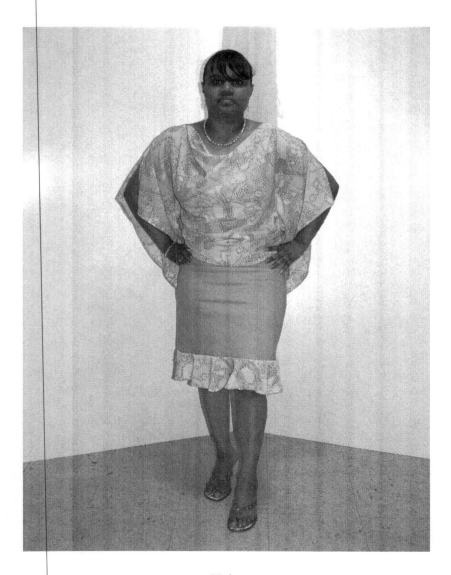

Tisha

Tisha